# HIS REAL LIFE

# His Real Life

CATHERINE HOFFMANN

RESOURCE *Publications* · Eugene, Oregon

HIS REAL LIFE

Copyright © 2014 Catherine Hoffmann. All rights reserved. Except for brief quotations in critical publications or reviews, no part of this book may be reproduced in any manner without prior written permission from the publisher. Write: Permissions. Wipf and Stock Publishers, 199 W. 8th Ave., Suite 3, Eugene, OR 97401.

Resource Publications
An Imprint of Wipf and Stock Publishers
199 W. 8th Ave., Suite 3
Eugene, OR 97401

www.wipfandstock.com

ISBN 13: 978-1-62564-871-6

Manufactured in the U.S.A.                                06/03/2014

This novel is dedicated to the Urantia Book

# Contents

*Chapter I*
A Bare Spot | 1

*Chapter II*
Growing | 7

*Chapter III*
John, Rebecca and the Zealots | 21

*Chapter IV*
A Pilgrim | 36

*Chapter V*
On the Road | 49

*Chapter VI*
Rome | 58

*Chapter VII*
The Return from Rome | 65

*Chapter VIII*
Ready | 78

*Chapter IX*
John | 84

*Chapter X*
Baptism and Forty Days | 91

*Chapter XI*
## His Friends | 100

*Chapter XII*
## Waiting in Galilee | 111

*Chapter XIII*
## A Man like This | 118

*Chapter XIV*
## Waiting | 130

*Chapter XV*
## The Ordination of the Twelve | 136

*Chapter XVI*
## This Bright Day | 149

*Chapter XVII*
## Until Him | 161

*Chapter XVIII*
## Holy Land: The Apostle's Epilogue | 166

*Chapter I*

# A Bare Spot

It's spring.
    In the new light, a boy, soon thirteen, walks with his father hand in hand. They pass beneath that most gentle of trees, the olive, their faces wattled by its shade. Hearing the hoof thuds of the ass on which his mother sat, the boy shot at her a quick look of fun. She was singing along with the others, sprigs of her hair flying free. How he loved that face! Blondish and bold, of essence as strong as the hand of the man he held.
    They were travelling in caravan along the Jordan valley. Here the boy saw the slim green Jordan winding from up North down to the Dead Sea. In the valley, warmth of a tropical, flower-laden kind perfumed their senses. The burnt-gold grain, clumps of pink oleander, snow-capped Mount Hermon aloft in the azure, and later, looking up that night, the rainbows of stars dancing. Such was the land they journeyed.
    At night the snoozers snored in their tents. Beside his parents, the boy lay on the ground. Looking up at the stars, he could hardly hold in the suspense. On the morrow he was to see it at last! The City of Heaven, Jerusalem! Tomorrow also, was his day of consecration, that point in him, as in anyone, boiling to be met. He was to be made a Son of the Law, to offer himself to the life-work in him. But what would that be? His mother, a woman of a grand patriotic assertion, had always had a vision of a destiny for him. But as he lay now in the intense spring dark, the boy had to ask was his consecration to God? Or to be a glory-son of the race? For Israel, the sacred people? The nation chosen by God?

The child turned on the ground. From the beginning, he had felt otherwise. From the blood in his veins he knew one fact; God could be a wind, a gale, a tree, a lamb, even a man, but could a nation be God? The creation was in everyone. Everything else followed from that. Though only a young thing, he knew about the light that yearned out of all life, knew that the One who made the light was a father, the Father of life. And that the Light of the World so awaited by his nation was the universal perspective, so it couldn't be only for the Jews, his own fold. And this was just one of the several reasons he thought his great and much loved mother was mistaken about anyone's being special in this, or any other world.

Their home was in Galilee. A thorny, bruise-colored land in winter, but come a wildflowering spring, and their hill town of Nazareth in a blaze of red poppies, became a slope of heaven. Theirs was a poor house. His father Joseph worked away at carpentry work. Mary made their home. She dug the garden, planted, hammered. Their off-white shack was half-way up that northern hill in sight of a flatland of juniper groves and cypresses. In their house they had the one room, a stone table in it, a mill for grinding corn out the back. The way to eat was to squat about the table, and they did, ravenous, enjoying their food, gouging out the dollops of garlicky chickpea. By his fifth year Mary had taught him how to care for vines and plants. He learnt to train the peas up the walls that ran around their plot like a white stone girdle. On the roof Mary organized sand boxes for him to learn to write and draw maps in them. But of all the best was the birth of the babies, his brothers and sisters. He stood around the baby cots looking on at their frolic and beauty, watching their antics for hours.

Life was happy. But there was his mother's face-of-expectation. The way Mary bent across his brothers and sisters, lifting the bowls of figs, offering him the first of the honey, the best of dates. He did not respond to any special care. Nor to that waiting in her eyes. He was relieved to start school where he now had a friend, Jacob, and where kids of all sorts meant so much more to him—and no, he didn't like that large reverential glitter in his mother's eyes when anyone even said the word "Yeshua"—the heck! It was just a name!

His favorite thing to do was to walk out with his father and climb that hill of Nazareth. Holding the hand of Joseph, the two of them used to climb to the top. From here the boy could see the whole world—well, that's how it felt. At the peak together, the man and boy saw Mount Tabor jutting out of the plain like a thumb. From here he saw the hills of Nain, the long, down-gliding ridge of Mount Carmel gliding into the sea. Looming out of the north was Mount Hermon's calm white brow. Where the sun rose was the Jordan Valley, the rocky hills of Moab in the far distance. And when Joseph and he turned to the down-going sun in the West, they could descry in the gloaming of distance the gold Mediterranean.

These years in the workshop of his father, Yeshua ben Joseph was mingling with the teeming flocks of humanity. Here he was learning to make reigns and straps. His mother he helped after school. A hotly-spoken, brilliant woman, Mary and he sparred together, they joked and jousted, they argued, they jeered, they sang. Sometimes he hugged and held her, and she, him.

He now recalled how in the February of his sixth year, while horsing around with Jacob, his friend, he had hidden in a wadi for a minute. It was the cool time—no flies, ah, the relief! —and he'd just darted behind a prickly pear, the life running in him, when he stopped. He looked up. A new focus had arrived. It had come, a steadying of consciousness. Soft in approach, his soul received its absolute focal point of God, the usual arrival of spirit, a gentle genesis of self.

If the boy looked midway into the air, then, as mildly at the ground, he would have seen there, it is certain, no sign. He heard no message, nothing outside nature at all. On that bare spot he saw only Palestine shale, rubbly bits, village debris, jags of stone. But when he looked up, he had come to resolve. Perhaps he made a decision to rejoin the game, come out of the shade in full view for Jacob, or to anyone, quietly, and in the future always, and anyhow.

By his seventh year he played the harp, spoke Greek nearly as well as their own homely Aramaic, could milk the cow, make cheese, work the loom. He talked often with his sisters. He was meeting the mothers and girls drawing water at the spring that served all Nazareth. A potter in town had given Jacob and him some clay to mold. The squelchy wonder stuff! Of *course* they were going to be potters when they grew up!

And next, this happened. Yeshua had done a heinous thing—a charcoal sketch of the village *chazzan*! Out over the hills stormed the school's deputies to their shanty on the village edge. They berated shy, tongue-tied father. Listening to the stentorian bellowing, his son resented their blaming of this melancholy man. Nor did he think an image you made really offended the Creator, after all, quite a Maker himself! and who, being such a hand at it, surely understood the passion for creation, having put it into humans in the first place. When he tried saying all this, his teachers turned purple in the face.

"How can you *know*?" they gasped.

"The truth in me says."

"*Your* truth!"

"No!" he, an uncontending boy, stood his ground for once, "Not just mine, the one as in everyone."

The men of authority made prune lips. They hooted at what the boy said. But his mother produced a hiss that sounded like "Zsssssttt!" at the fools, casting derisive bolts from her thunderously beautiful brown eyes. Her son would be brilliant, Mary now knew, and folded her magnificent Amazonian arms; she knew it in her bones!

The rebukers left. But his father Joseph only turned to him in that minimal way he had. "Never draw again, son. Do you understand?"

Blazing at authority before, now his boy only said, "It shall be as you say."

Every Sabbath they used to go walking, the two of them, unpossessively, hand-in-hand. They climbed the mimosa-yellow hill near their home for that dear, cosmic panorama. They traipsed across Nazareth's rolling terrain, tackling the higher tracks, asking and replying to each other's questions about people, about events, and nature. In the May of his eighth year he was sent to his uncle's farm in Magdala. It was the first time Yeshua ben Joseph saw the ancient Lake Chinnereth. It was almost a sea, the Sea of Galilee. At the glimpse of it, his breath fled. That out-of-this-world astonishing lake, the force of air around it, the upward rush of earth from its sides like an avalanche in reverse. In spring the lake's shoreline was white with almond groves framed by tender blue hills. Capernaum below was a perfect, salt white city by the sea. There was a moment the boy heard the landscape reply to a driving question he had; "What is *for* the soul?"

When he looked out on the shining masses of water, the trees and air, he could see it, and say, "This. *This!*"

An un-noisy boy, light of heart, and yet, the people of Nazareth had started buzzing about him. Attention, the last thing he wanted, was coming to him. But why? A quality in him so at home in the world that it made him seem strange. Yet, his style was plain. He spoke clearly. His words were sparse. He stood at ease and looked you level in the eye as he reasoned, inviting you to track along with him. His mind was given to see what there really was out there, then to tally it with what lived within. His face full of immensities, there was a light play about him too, but no will to win, just a willingness to go anywhere thought led. And that on-the-brink laugh of his, to become a helpless roar, he was very funny at times, so he infuriated some people. And another thing, that half-curl of a smile of his. It did not bid well in a land where the dignity of a male was that he be solemn, stubborn, asserting in unbudgeable whites and blacks. Yeshua's smile disconcerted the dull and the serious. The careful he riled. The prudent he seemed to vex. The stingy fat kids of complacent cast, and the needy, boneless mama-boys resented that he was lithe, smelt clean as the desert, that he laughed a lot and needed absolutely nothing from anyone. Decent people were galled by a laugher like that. But a few others liked him, that tiger energy of a sunny boy, free and apart. The least defended loved him, particularly young children, and even more, the foolish gladsome girls of hilarious heart.

His mother spoke to him of his cousin, the far-away John. Though John lived leagues distant in the Judean desert, Yeshua knew him somehow. His cousin was an untamed boy, his nature of the purity of ancient Israel from when Jews had loved the Lord in the desert with a virgin heart. But Israel came out of the desert, lost its virginity to the power of the city, to the authority of rulers, kings and priests, to the snobbery of castes and sects. Like a wild tree, his cousin John would live on in the desert, its branches open, but only to God. When people spoke of John, Yeshua knew, they were, the both of them, just waiting.

One day, a Rabbi called Nahor came to Nazareth. The *Rebbe* was to sound out the lad for a much proposed career of Rabbi in Jerusalem. Yeshua was to become, local opinion implied, a person of religious renown. He would do a deed for his nation from a platform of note, either as an anointed Son, or a warrior redoubtable. A few on the fringe even mumbled about him being the one to set the holy nation back to former glories and strength, while he, their boy Yeshu, he only wanted to sit in a boat and fish! Or even more, just to be with the sea, and the folk of the shore. He wanted to be with everyone somehow. He told the Rabbi of this ambition, not very well-formed.

Nahor, the pious man, was shocked. The spineless vagueness, the wishy-washiness! —yet somehow . . . the presumption of what this smiler-boy said! And, far more seriously, this "everyone" was a foreign conceit. In Israel's national self-confirmation expressions like "Others" and "Together" were laughable, if not actually treacherous.

In a world like that, were Yeshua to say a word about a God who, being a Father, loved everyone, he would have scandalized them all. So he held his tongue.

Then once, strolling on Nazareth's hills with his father, the huge paw of the workman around his hand, he spoke for the first time of what was going on in him. In a boy-voice he spoke for the first time of himself to Joseph. Last year, it was in June, wasn't it? —when they had climbed Mount Tabor together and it was as if they were looking not only on the land of Judah and Ephraim but on the entire world.

Joseph lowered his head. In the shade he adjusted his mantle. And listened.

As the two of them finned down Nazareth's slopes of low-hanging pines, his boy spoke of becoming aware of a life, a doing in himself.

Joseph stood by, his skin going pale. But he heard out his son in the pine tree's spindly shade. And said nothing.

Perhaps it was two years ago, his son was saying, when this sense first presented itself. There weren't any right words for it, or, he couldn't find them, and words couldn't do everything, could they? But a thing now present to him at all times, well, to a part of him, was an image unfurling of a wholeness, as of a universe itself. No, it wasn't voices, he wasn't hearing any. And he could stop it any time, he had in fact limited, emptied himself from knowing it. Still, he could make it come, all the clarity for life a human needed, it would all stand up and come forth from within.

But, he said, he wished for his life to go in the ordinary channel of its natural human flowing.

"So, you see," he turned to his Joseph father, "I can't talk of it, not really." And when he smiled that young breaking smile of a child's helplessness, his father Joseph knew; his first boy, now in his eleventh year, was entering torment.

*Chapter II*

# Growing

At school he learnt well. At synagogue he spoke when asked. He listened to Nazareth's rabbis, took rote from the *chazzan*, ran around with children. But what he liked most was to listen to folks from the road, the roadsters who had lived a lot, and looked like it. All of life was coming at him, a huge tide of beings with whom he wanted to live. The wave of a world desire was surging in him, along with the certainty of its clash with the wishes of his parents. They were the ones he loved, loved more than everyone else, but, and he knew this, all his doing wouldn't be for them.

He liked too, the farm at Magdala, liked the quirky fish in the sea, the flinty ground, the budding of grass, his mother's mattock, the sound it made when she hammered the lilium stakes in. And there was Jacob, his friend, who was quite a heft. Jacob was his champion at school when kids jibbed him with names like "Yesh" and "Shu" and quite a few things else. When they picked on him, Jacob would stomp up to the pack and administer those wallops which he, Yeshu, somehow hadn't. Once, the kids put burrs in his hair, and he sort of scream-laughed. Another time he got stung raw by the stinging nettles they rubbed on his back. Next in the routine, the brats put briers on his seat, the thorns gashing him when he sat, but he only cried an involuntary "Whoooops!" and didn't curse, or anything. The tough boys said he was weak. He, of course, paid no mind to dents to his dignity like that. Having James and Jacob to play with, Martha, and Miri, and Simon, and now also baby Jude newly arrived! He, Yeshua, was running around the world in a skin-to-skin fit with his tearing-around, happy life.

But there was his mother's love. Once a spritely, singing girl, now weathering into a stately beauty, Mary's passion remained for her own, be they her children, her family, her proud genealogy of race. But the central nerve of Mary's passion was him, her first born son. He was so exclusively hers, why, for all that her man Joseph had contributed to this conception, Mary might have been a virgin, that is, solo, in giving life to her prime and superb son. The way her eyes would slow on him, and stop, caused him to wonder, did Mary know something about him that he didn't? So then, why didn't he ask? Perhaps he knew enough of how to be, and wanted to make his own destiny, and with no extra help. In fact, at times he had a sense of knowing so much that he made himself deliberately void, even stupid, so as to not know it. Yet his mind was ordinary, not slow, nor lightning quick. But it had no impediments. His was a plain mind of no warps or cramps, or any of the self-imposed hurdles about the fantastic perfections dreamt up by narcissistic boys. He was a straight-ahead young person who loved, so God was there, prime source, and self-evident. But the thing he couldn't work out these years was—how do you live true to what you are, and stay loyal to mother and father, life's givers, the givers of life?

When he was eleven, with Joseph they went to the Decapolis cities. Though Joseph kept himself deaf to it, people spoke that shapeliest of languages there. The forms the mouth had to make in the utterance of Greek were more noble and flexuous, if less dear, than their old home Aramaic. Though a builder, his father refused to see, let alone marvel the white beauty of the Greek temples. Joseph kept an averted silence through his son's carols of delight at pediment and frieze, at the columns, fluted or carved. When the boy looked at a Greek temple, power, grace and mathematics came to mind. Games were on in the amphitheatre. Bare limbed youths were perforating the sky itself with athletic leaps and bounds. Everywhere was a neigh of laughter, a flexing of energy, effort, finesse. Joseph's boy clapped his hands for joy. Life's spice ran in his blood. He laughed at the stunts, the humor, the camaraderie of sports. "Oh! Father!" he jumped for the fun, "Let's build an amphitheatre in Nazareth!"

Joseph's face turned black. "What an evil thought." He, a pious Jew had to say, "Never let it into your mind."

"Very well," said the child by his side, but with respect.

Then the man saw; his boy would do anything out of loyalty to them. For this reason Joseph made up his mind: bring no judgments for this son; let his nature develop freely, know what it would, of itself.

But the boy was learning discretion. Because he had begun to see, and with no pleasure, that yes, he *was* different. It wasn't as if he was clear about his own nature. Of his work in the world, even less. All he knew was the oddness was there. Where other boys more gifted than he might flaunt a difference, he was learning to hide everything that might separate him from others.

That year was a clash of values with vision.

And again there was Mary. She could not do enough for him. So he was drawing further back. On the straw floor with his sleeping siblings at nights, it was impossible not to hear his mother talk with his father in hoarse, stabbing whispers. Mary's thought was all about him, her favorite son. Her will for him was to achieve a distinction of a national kind. At least Joseph had the good sense to say nothing to that. Or just to make a small murmur to the effect, that their boy's fate might after all be only spiritual. A rift with Mary was developing. It upset the family. And it hurt Mary's emotion for the Lord's great people, Israel. She was stung in her ancestral pride, that, indeed, including illustrious Ruth, Anise, Bathsheba, Tamar, though Mary's more immediate culture was somewhat Phoenician, Greek and Hittite. Her son's drifting from her hurt Mary's pride of belonging to the people of the Lord's chosen favor. And worse, it questioned Mary's prime experience—that unforgettable sundown when enclosing her own shape in her arms, she folded over as the envoy of the Lord held out a hand to her, and said,

"Mary, the conception within you is ordained by Heaven. The Lord of all earth shall overshadow you. Our benediction upon you."

There had never been, or would ever be again, anything like that.

When Mary told her husband about the angel's decree of Heaven's purpose, Joseph fell quiet. He restrained all judgment. He held it back. But he was troubled. Then he had a dream which distinctly said, "To as many as shall receive him shall he reveal they are God's child." And when the infant arrived, he was so lovely that it was enough, and nothing else mattered.

Shortly after the visitation, Mary journeyed south to her older kinswoman, Elizabeth who dwelt in the village City-of-Judah, not far from Jerusalem. A few months ago, in Elizabeth too, a late conception had taken. Under the trees of the Judean village the two mothers greeted each other with marvelling cries. Taking a brown-blond sprig of Mary's hair in her fingers, Elizabeth had said, "My own child shall be, the celestial visitor told me, 'The forerunner of the Soul-Healer.'"

"So my child will be the Messiah?" Mary, embarrassing Elizabeth, had cried.

"No!" her much older kinswoman waved Mary down like a foolish girl, "The Messiah is but a dream of Israel! Your child shall be the deliverer of the world!"

But for Mary her "Child of Promise" was to become the restorer of her race. And like most human beings of her zone, Mary couldn't imagine what could possibly be meant by "the World," or its "Deliverance," unless, it meant the re-instating of God's chosen people to former power. For was the first fruit of his loins and receiver of the Lord's most special blessing not Israel?

After all, so said sacred Scripture.

About the boy.

As perhaps in any child, there were two streams of knowledge in him. One was a cosmic flow of information, the other, his own personal awareness. The two streams ran parallel but did not meet in him yet. He trusted one day they would. He tried making little of this two-fold flow, a bifurcation of his nature, and therefore of some trouble to him. From his times with Joseph on the hill, his identity had gone on developing. For now, it was enough that he was here, learning what it was to be alive, to be God's, and still a child. But on that other level, he knew, what he had in him was a task of no precedent. Though it wasn't any special possession of God—everyone had that—it was somewhat the reverse; it was a work about how the Father was to be shared, made manifest. This was his one clear personal orientation. That he knew of no one with such a call, made Yeshua, not glow, or feel special, but appalled. Otherwise a jocular boy, it made him neither dreamy nor mystical—he would never be that—but left him with a love unmanageable, you couldn't curb, control or reason about it. So he felt isolated.

And therefore alone. Times were he would catch his mind yearning towards a person, just the one human to whom he could speak. In these desirous states he would turn to an imagined friend with such a longing to be heard that it embarrassed him.

Much of time would be a waiting, he sensed. So from the strung-out anguish of the time lag he turned to God, the basis of himself. Like a plant to the sun, like a son to his Father, it was a turning to Source, a going to roots in order to reach for the love of what lived in him. He had an instant, natural grasp of the origin and end that was God, if an unclear grasp of himself. All he knew was, he was a son, a creature like anyone else, and also that he contained in potential a whole universe. As far as he could, he bridled thoughts like that. To the conventional child that he also was, they made no sense. And because they made him far too other from every person, a difference he didn't want. But whenever this dire truth-grasp came, it went on shaping and forming, rending, but also as if to join his divided selves.

What rescued him was interest in people. He was saved from strangeness by engaging with the world's issues and frictions. Now, take the Temple's priests! How they shut out the poor, the infirm and the lame, all excluded from Israel's salvation. It was clear, and surely to anyone, a human being wasn't what you could see or say about them. People weren't their pasts! They were God's, and had a future that was limitless, with lives to be made, chosen and lived, and in a love without bounds.

Another nonsense that riled anyone who thought was the priest's resorting to oral law whenever it suited them! They made up customs, then called them "Law" when they couldn't explain something. Take that trite thing of finger-touching at the door-post's *mezuzah*, a box said to contain the first letter of God's name! He was repulsed by the fake piety of superstition and all habitual obeisance. *This* was the idolatry—with a wrench he re-felt that sacrifice in his past—not the images of art! For was art not a praise, a longing for God? Or, so he would have argued. But he did not contend, slow to defend his rights, at this time still quite dulcet and docile of nature.

This day in April their group was on the Passover pilgrimage to Zion's center, the city, Jerusalem. They sang psalms in the vernal air as they journeyed across hills springy with flowers. The sun shone. The earth teemed. The whole of the land heaved and shone, a garden of Heaven. Across the plains the wind bore scents of life and loam to his senses. They wound on in pilgrim company in the white air of the Judean wilderness, its terrain, an intestinal magma spewed up from the open gashes of earth.

They were entering Jericho, a low, hot place. Here, his father Joseph re-told him the fable of the Joshua after whom he, Yeshua, was named. As to all the sacred stories, he listened, reverential, rapt. But he was holding the love for the peak moment of all, that long-awaited glimpse of Jerusalem.

Their caravan passed the old sanctuaries of Bethel and Shiloh. They trudged on, bowing to the tombs of the prophets, many of them, in that land of bloodied absolutes, stoned to death. Jewry's love had always had a noose around it; everything outside the self-affirming circle of its own community was a void. At a time when several of the world's peoples had already placed their highest good into an unknown truth yet to come, what the children of Abraham did not know did not exist for them. The prophets had long broken through this constricting ring, hollering at Israel to open its heart to the stranger, and had mostly perished for it. Yet these prophets were the true spirit of Israel. On passing their tombs, Yeshua bowed his head and touched his heart to them, recalling the ancients with reverence as their fragile human caravan vanished into the ferocious sunset over the rocky sands of Judea.

Next day they were pushing upwards. Reaching plateau, the land unrolled. Through the blue-hazed wastes of the Judean desert they went. Close to the hamlet of Bethany, their exhausted uphill grappling group paused to rest. From the yards villagers were pouring out with ladles of water for the pilgrims, slices of watermelon. A family approached Yeshua's family, three children in tow. As the parents hooked arms and gossiped by the road, their boy, Lazarus, began with Yeshua a straightaway chat. The girl Martha, brandished at him a fistful of real Egyptian dates, then plopped them, one by one in his palm. Making the chuckly noises of thanks, Yeshua now turned to the youngest, a skinny child with a wide open face. This girl was Mary, an adoring type, the sort to love things for existing, just that they did. Perhaps Mary always loved, but never knew what loved her back, she supposed, say, maybe a tree, or a gorgeous fat cat, or maybe an unlikely shower of rain in the month of Nissan. But in Bethany now, on looking Yeshua clear in the eye, Mary's random adorings gathered to a point, peaked, then rushed at her. An awkward, uncontrolling child, on looking at him, she turned a wild poppy red. For she saw; it wasn't a diffuse "What" that loved Mary; a "what" can't do that! It was a Who that loved Mary first, a person, a universal person she saw in Yeshua, or, whoever was the One he stood for. Smiling helplessly at being delivered of pantheistic silliness, Mary was glad to know love was of persons. Focused somehow, she didn't feel all over the place or scattered anymore.

And now the four children dived into an embroiling sea of serious subjects, teasing points and banter. Martha, a square chinned girl, pulled her sister's raven black plait. She put on a voice, "Since babyhood Mary's been a fantast!"

"An exaggerator!" Lazarus moderated it.

And the four laughed because it was all well meant. But when Yeshua looked at Mary, a girl accused of fantasy, later to become a woman of almost clairvoyant beauty, he said, "Maybe Mary will be a poet, of the soul!" They laughed some more, conversed and walked about, talking of Jerusalem. Yeshua's new friends saw a career of excellence for him there. Though all he said was, he wasn't sure if to be a rabbi was what was meant. Before parting, the children touched one another's shoulders lightly and knew; what had happened was a friendship for life.

The pilgrims continued. Their caravan wound up the last slope of Bethphage. As they scaled the shoulder of Mount Olivet, it hove into view—the awaited sight! Even without the other's shouts of pious delight, Yeshua recognized it, zoned in rings of light, the intense beauty of the city of Zion. The vision of Jerusalem shook him, the tiers of rock, Mount Moriah and Mount Mitspe, the far courts of the Temple to the Father, the colossal architectural execution and grandeur of it all in a smoky rose light.

They went down and into it.

That night, in the house of friends, his mother Mary was ensconced in chat. There was a merry ado over the Passover's seating, the foods, the songs. His father sat, dark and recessive to the one side, inclining his head to the usual house-chat—humiliated national glory and its resurgence. Yeshua missed his brothers and sisters, each farmed out to kinsfolk back in Galilee. Himself the eldest, too petted and praised, he went off to where he always did at such times; to be by himself. Outside the house, he was inside the night, faced to the high walled garden. He plunked down on a lump of flat stone. He swung his legs. Looking up, and out, the scrubbed lunar slopes of Jerusalem were visible over the marl white fence. The hills formed a circle centering the minds of those within. A magnetic place, the way Jerusalem pulled you center, it turned you inward, in. Above the cool rock where he sat, the sparse leaves of a carob etched their dim, unassuming shapes on the silence. Though it was the deep of night the lilac aureole of dusk still lingered. As the boy looked above to the blue sky-spaces studded with the stars of the universes whirling above, he found upon an in-rush of amazement, but of no surprise, that he knew them, knew them all! By name and nature, and with love.

As the circles of Jerusalem's hills came in close, he felt his mind shift, re-arrange itself, then divide. And what he never before grasped began to converge, gathering in him to a point. So, he stood up. For an instant nothing happened. Then time stopped. And matter cracked. Space opened. And stepping outside into the universe, he was walking inside of himself.

What, he asked, is the Universe? And found he knew, knew the created whole of it, all, and at once and straightaway.

The Grand Universe was a gigantic wheel of worlds. Seven spokes of creation formed the wheel, each, a radiation of Spirit, each a Superuniverse. All seven spokes, the boy looked upon the recognized splendor, as it moved in a processional swing around the First Source and Center, who was—this was known always—his own Source.

Ours, it sped in rapidly on him, was a Superuniverse. In its gravity clasp were many universes. One of them, a small one, was where he now dwelt, and of which—the occlusion shifted as the infinite field in him became clear—he was its Creator.

"Am I?" clouding over again, the child asked in the night.

Then, he asked what everyone does, and must sometime answer for themselves, "Who am I?"

As he looked within, the answer came of itself: I am one who has lain down my lines of power to be a human child of time and space. I am here to share the human state as a helper, to take humans back to who they are. I come, not to be an idol for God, but to embody the Father-presence of God, that humans may know him, and who they, themselves, are.

"And no," it dawned in him with a smile of greeting like a light, "I am not God, the Absolute Creator who ordained the universes, but a Son. I am the Son-phase of God to this world of space-time, a brother to all the loved ones of this planet. I," it went on processing in him, "am the personality of God that can be known by Man. I am a Son-of-God, a Brother to this world for humans."

Now the boy sat. He sat blank, on a stone. He was doing nothing anymore. He had no emotion at being shown himself. He had absorbed it with his whole being. But this was not the end, only the start. He was to go now, and grow to it, earn its full consciousness. What he was, it was so tremendous, yet there wasn't a trace now of the unusual on his face. For he was still a child, still of Palestine, still a son of Israel. And tomorrow was still the day he would be received into the consensus of the Covenant. Looking ahead, he was quite settled again to the human wave as one of the frequencies of himself. Tomorrow would be a day of avowal and pact, of family pride, that is, of delusion; a stoking of his father Joseph's uncertainties and of his mother's nationalist hopes. And once again he was very hungry. From the outside kitchen in the garden he helped himself to some wafers of unleavened bread. Presented at last with who he was, he ate as naturally, with the eager sobriety as might anyone on having at last contacted themselves.

He brushed his mouth of the whitish flakes of crumbly flat bread. Stepping out into the April garden once more, he would have gone now into the night to walk under its stark dark beauty by himself. But in the floodtide of silent illumination he was moved with a desire to pray—when through the dark a spiral of light evolved, fleshed out, then bowed in greeting. "I am of Immanuel, your Paradise brother," as in an immanence of no sound spoke the flesh of light, "And I am to tell you, the time has come."

Yeshua, the child, knelt. He was neither shocked nor frightened by the celestial emanation, having always had the knowledge of this in a part of himself. He knelt now to bring himself and his hands together before the point always converging in him. And listened. "The time?" he respectfully asked.

"The time," spoke the light, "to be about the Father's business."

That was all. And it was over.

When the boy stood up on the garden's gravely ground, it was with the proper weight of the universe settling into himself.

Of course, everything changed after that. What happened at this Passover did not disturb him. He had always pre-known it, had long ago agreed to it, had chosen it in fact. Its epiphany was only a manifestation of the fact. So it made no difference, well hardly any. This event had been supernatural, from a plane of reality not to re-open to him for an age. The entire event was to become a mere wave of memory in him, unconfirmed, fading, often in doubt. He would retain the uncertainty of his identity, not then knowing the massive effort to become fully conscious of it, not until a long time from now. His work to perfect his own self-understanding was to be the story of consciousness itself. His journey to his identity was to be so psychologically exact, that, like most people, he wouldn't exactly know what he was, not until nearly at the end of his life. Only towards the close of it, when knee-deep in a muddy brown river under humid palms, having given himself quite over to God, would he receive his identity's full scope.

In Jerusalem the following day, Yeshua ben Joseph entered the temple.

It was phenomenal. Hewn of gigantic, massive stone, the structure shone bronze, pewter, fawn, depending on the light. Right inside was the Holy of Holies, the sanctum of dark emptiness, a sign for where God dwelt. But as his mother let go his hand and sheered off to take her place in the women's gallery, he almost burst out, "What's the justice of a woman separated in worship from men?" He half imagined his mother suffering at the derogation of it, but Mary was smiling through a yawn, and indifferent, blunted by the long habit of it, justified as "religion."

The service began. At that first second, the noise that hit his ear was perfectly incredible. A flailing, frenzied, ear-cudgelling chant. The worshippers eyes glazed-over—to whom exactly were they yowling? —mouths twisting from side to side, bodies jerking in a back-and-forth neural spasm. The din revved up, rose to a roar to stop you from having one single thought of God. His hands rose to his head. He held onto himself like that, enduring it. Step by onerous step, he was rotated through the rituals, dismayed by their hysterical or routine nature. He had hoped perhaps for silence, for a pure symbol, a whispered poetry of prayer with an intimate-to-soul resonance. Not this hawking, sputtering, squawking yammering of absurdities—an affront to Heaven.

Later, when he tried to ask about it, he received replies that were puerile, even to a child. With his parents he walked for the first time in the courts of the Father's temple, trying to let no one see how his innocence was torn. His hopes crushed as he watched the money-lenders and courtesans strut their ware of flesh, their faces askew and deepening with emptiness. Much worse than the sale of sex, was the holler of "Money!" "Money!" "Money!" the exploitative, excited cheapness of it. And what—it touched him with the claw of panic—what was that stench? It oozed everywhere, a thick reek, not just of wild fur, burnt hooves and bone, but a rot of nature turned against itself. It was horrible. Holding onto his father's hand, when they came to the priests' court he saw the cause of the smell. Animals howling in horror, defecating in terror. Droves of terrified beasts were being wedged into vices, rammed onto stakes by the blood red hands of priests. He saw the necks of lambs being slit or hacked, the skin opening, blood geysers spurting, viscera falling out. He heard the smaller beasts squeal, their horrific death cries as their lives passed into gagging river of gore in floods of blood.

He wanted to vomit.

*Growing*

Grabbing the sleeve of Joseph's coat, he buried his face in it as any notion of Jerusalem's holiness guttered out in the horror scream of dying animals.

After the slaughter, the sludge of wrecked tissue and body parts, the rivers of blood offered to the Father of Heaven, and the boy was neither withdrawn, nor snapped shut; he had to speak to them! As a Son of the Covenant he was free to do so and entitled to move about alone in the temple. So he went to the courts of discussion. He was to make his thoughts into words for others so he would put it to them; why would Heaven's Father be appeased by blood? How could the Creator demand the blood of blameless beasts for human error? His Jewish brethren from the globe's four corners present, Yeshua first tried listening to the obsessive disputations, the casuistic, fribbling, word-splitting debates. But when he put his hand up to be heard, as a son of the consecration it was his right, the man next to him whacked his own face—the effrontery!—this snip of a boy, presuming to speak! And the adjudicator didn't allow it. But Yeshua stayed on, persistent, quietly, thinking of all he had seen.

He had lost sight of his parents a while ago. No matter, he thought, they would turn up. All day he walked about, or sat with chin in his hands. He was thinking. Since the temple's destruction more than half a millennium ago, Jewry had seen itself as maimed. To the acquisitive spirit, the loss of rule and land was felt as annihilation, the loss of life itself. The temple's leaders had turned their land-loss into the land-cult of Zion, a political movement. The Hebrew anguish at territory take-over was enshrined in the Temple, a shibboleth for a turning-to-God. For those at the helm of authority in Israel, power was territory, land and property, all disguised as a longing for Jewish identity, which too, was meant to be a command from God. The land-cult of Zion had made of an ordinary people a Sacred Nation, of an ordinary patch of territory a "holy land." The Temple was an emblem of Israel's profane history, a hodgepodge of invasions, vengeances, cruelty, rapacity and bitterness, all written over by the priests of the exile in Babylon, a history falsified into being "sacred." The temple exuded the blood-pride of the race. And it grieved Yeshua, a pile of proud stones, void of love or spirit.

Afternoon passed. Still no sight of his parents. He didn't see them anywhere. In the evening he climbed a hill of Jerusalem and from the top sauntered down to shrubby Bethany, to the house of his friends Mary, Martha and Lazarus. Unworried, he slept there that night, sure his parents would come sometime. He wasn't anxious. In this he was strange, perhaps. He felt at home in any place. He ate anything. He could sleep wherever. He spoke with anyone, at home in his skin, and in the world, under the stars and God.

Next day at the temple the air was still rent by the wail of animals. His head in his hands through the noise, Yeshua sat on the seats of stone. Alone a lot of the time that Passover week, he was trying to work out how to say—the death of animals could not possibly be asked by God as ransom for sin, a purchase by sacrifice. If only humans could think out what sin is, why we are born, and who God actually was!

Each night of his first Passover, as later in his most human of times, he was to sleep at the Bethany house of his friends. Unaware that his parents had left Jerusalem—they were already in Jericho in fact—he supposed they were busy socializing. He had a basic faith in humans, and trusted his ability to fend for himself. As for Mary, Martha, and Lazarus, the pact of friendship with his Bethany three already felt it would be forever. The thing was the four really liked one another. Martha, a homely, obliging girl was, while discerning, ready to like anyone. Mary, an intense child, had a mystery of some deep capacity about her. And Lazarus was a warm natured boy of the times. From the keeping of company with him, Lazarus had a sense that Yeshua, his friend, would achieve invincibility by the simple ardor of his goodness. It would only be the inert, self-satisfied boys who might not like Yeshua, saying he was familiar, or too casual, when it was a pure gaiety and gladness about him much of the time.

A day or so later, Yeshua did wonder when his parent Joseph would find him. But at that moment in the Temple, he was granted the right to speak at last. About to take his chance, he got up with glad, good humor. But wanting to outwit no one at all, he sat down again and asked his questions, from an easy, you might say, friendly posture of a young friend. As the boy began to form his idea, at the sound of his voice people began to crane their necks. They were just about to let themselves hear, his questions being the very ones knocking at Jewry's heart. Questions like: Why are women segregated in the worship of God? If God loves his children, why slaughter animals? Why the barter and trade in the temple of Heaven's Lord? What of the awaited Messiah—was he to be a temporal prince on David's throne, or was he the Light of Life to come out of Israel to establish a new way of relations with God through the soul?

Those beginning to hear him were astonished. The boy's phrasing, its challenge, and that lovely child-eagerness to hear what they said. The endearing way he sat with the elders—the boy seemed to have no desire for logical triumph—just to be there, and with them. And when he spoke he did not assume the hectoring, declamatory stand, but stayed seated amidst the Temple's teachers, the elders patting his hands, others, leaning to a pillar as they listened, smiling to the heart. A few crusty old Jews listening to him there looked on moist-eyed, blessed to be hearing, the long unheard presentation of Israel's true fruit. But a few were piqued by it. Why, he was just a boy! And from lowly Nazareth! From heathen Galilee! Not yet thirteen! How dare he talk!

But just as more people were beginning to feel what he said, a woman's cry cut the flow. At the key moment when this new Son of the Law was at last to be heard, Mary, his mother, rushed up. She pushed aside the listening crowd, and crushed to herself the boy who was speaking, him, Yeshua, her own boy! "What! O what have you done to us?" her vibrato upbraided him in moist, lacerated cries, "What have you done to your parents, my child?"

In the lush extravagance of her pain, Mary thought nothing of scotching the most serious effort of his young life. No, Mary a-flood in a welter of mother-feeling, thought nothing of his own purposes at all. Her hurt was greater. She and Joseph had searched for their son in Jericho, and three days back here in Jerusalem. And now on the surge of relief, she was not to stop and consider if there could be a matter greater to him than being his mother's child. Though the rapt look in the eye of the elders renewed in Mary her certainty about her son. Assuredly, he was to be the leader of the Holy People, a patriotic hero, at least a *zaddik* of Zion!

Publicly subverted and chided, her son took it well. Thwarted, he bowed to his parents. "Did you not know," under the circumstances his reply was mild, "that I would be in the Father's house?"

As the Nazareth family left the Temple, those who noted the gracious ring of the boy's words at his public humiliation by his mother, looked on long after them.

When the family reached the peak of Olivet, the city's panorama hove into view. Their son looked out on Jerusalem. A locus of Israel's exaltation, fanaticism, legal pedantry and religious spite, from Jerusalem might issue a spirit to ravage not only Palestine's green land but fanaticize the earth. A hub of Semitic blood-pride, of bondage to custom, Jerusalem's mood was apoplectic at being yoked to Rome. But it wasn't their political enslavement to Rome, but his people's obsession with power that was tormenting their souls. Israel had no spiritual religion, but one of tribal eminence. And the humiliation by Rome made them howl for a collective revenge. Jerusalem lived in a fit of wrath at Hebrew power being in foreign hands. He knew the way out. It was so simple, anyone might. But his saying it would earn him death. Entirely helpless, and hardly more than a child, he turned to the city, opened to it his arms.

"O Jerusalem," on the side of Olivet the boy shook as he said it, "How I would free you."

*Chapter III*

# John, Rebecca and the Zealots

Joseph taught him carpentry. He was learning about timber and metal, how you worked it, what it was. At synagogue he learnt Scripture. From school, mathematics, custom and lore. And from the coming of his brothers and sisters he was learning more about the sheer abundance, the generosity of God.

But if new lives were a sign of God's creative self-giving, their priest-run religion of diet and strictures, a legion of nit-picking regulations, was a frittering away of life itself. Israel's rulers were fixated on Law. To be religious was a political act. Turning to the God of Israel was an act of national self-definition by which you set yourself apart. What Yeshua feared for his people was if you reject the humanity that is your matrix, your soul's connection to the world will perish.

Himself of Judaic legacy, Yeshua never set himself apart from it. What he wished was for the Jewish spirit to include the foreigner and the stranger to the point these words of scare and abuse lost their meaning. He wished Israel's prayer to include the one thing left out; the equal love of God for all.

How to say this to his people? How to even hint that Heaven's Father was never compulsion, exclusion, or wrath, but the Maker of, not only Israel but of all the much-loved creatures, each with lives as precious as the infants he saw coming from his parents . . .

Such were the deepest matters in his thirteenth year.

And that his sweet and last little brother, Amos was born. Yeshua played the harp for Amos, a wan and sickly child, to cheer him up. Also by now, he was inventing stories, their characters, a lion, a leaf-toed gecko, a stripe-dressed bee. They were adventurous tales, quirky and funny, but always pondersome. At the caravan shop he was reciting his fables with a zippy young brio. Passers-by stopped. They peered around to the nook where he worked. They stayed a while, just listening to the boy.

Everybody was liking him. After that episode with Jerusalem's elders, Nazareth was taking note, sideways glances, as to a Son of Promise. Yeshua ben Joseph seemed to emerge with the winsome power of a youth of sturdy beauty and compelling mien. As he walked in the village, carrying, say, a slab of wood, or a hunk of leather, the eyes of a waiting generation were searching him with hope. From Israel's shame of bondage to Rome, those looking to him saw a free-striding lad becoming a contained and cheerful young man, blessed with a centrality of self-possession, or even a vision able to lead them out of tyranny. Revered old men would look at him with that intense Jewish longing in their eyes. They bent their ear to him when he spoke. There was a buzz, a whisper about him, like that Eastern yen for miracle always lazing about, and people began to ask, "Could he be the one for whom Israel longs? Even, maybe, the *Messiah*!"

And what about him? He was trying to see it—himself on a war-horse? A Davidic War-Lord? Wielding a sword? Judging the nations? Smiting the abominables? Why now—*was* that silly! The boy running across the blond paddock with hay had to bend double as he laughed. Seriously, he really did love his people, and since that sight of Jerusalem, first making him shout, then cry, he wanted to do something, but for everyone. Yet when he thought of that doing, it was not to launch apocalypse, but to say something about getting your mind fit, your soul open and limber for life. Though right now, for all the furious gestation of capacity in him, his task was to wait. And if to wait was miserable, he made himself do it; for waiting was also a doing, a work.

As he grew, his center of feeling was of being held by God. He found God everywhere he went. Involved with others, he had no interest, or, only moderately, in himself. All his devising was for people, for what he could do for them. He had no sense of himself as placed above anyone. His only difference was his future function. All he now knew was, when he began the work it would let him take his place more clearly with them. In no way did he feel himself a different kind of being. Nor did he wish to be. And if the struggle for his identity was to be long, and a trouble, it was also bearable since no value was found alone, but together with others.

*John, Rebecca and the Zealots*

From Joseph he had learnt to make chairs. Tables followed, then cabinets, things of sturdy use. And the shop's customers were watching Yeshua with pleasure. And also now—what to make of this one? —the eyes of girls. Even Ezra, his teacher at synagogue was saying, "Yeshua! I know it! You will be a leader!" And Joseph was setting money aside for his studies in Jerusalem. He was to start when he turned fifteen. The pious of the land had a fixed idea that a prophet performed miracles to prove his power; but from his own hand not one wonder had sprung. And though he did want to help, do his all for people, he didn't want to over-awe, had no wish to exceed, or to command. He wanted to do the one thing only, point to the truth behind the world, and pass it on.

When Yeshua thought of his own, the Jewish people, his pulse lurched with love. As his teacher, old Ezra once said, "There is a universal law; the degree of quality equals the degree of reality." This law, Ezra had said, was operative in the Jews. They were a quality folk of a high reality degree, a people who had a long way of loving God, searing, sacrificial, passionate. But Israel's love burnt only for its own. And this tore Yeshua. He would have lead them from this passion of exclusivity, out of themselves, free to the happiness of being at-one with humanity.

Then, his fourteenth year was one of embarrassment. As his mother continued watching him with that old self-enchanted pride, he found himself more in his father's company, such a muted, unassuming man, Joseph.

Yeshua was on the verge of a physically favored young manhood. The village was in a pother of augury about his fate. Ardent to meet all of possibility, in his fifteenth year Yeshua let this, a good boy's most tempting proposition into his head: might he still be the deliverer of the Jewish people? Could it be his to sit on the throne of David? To lead armies? Claim victory with the sword? Was he, according to Messiah legends, to raise the dead who had died? Was he, as Messiah, to lift the Holy City nine miles into the sky? To free Judea from ignominious occupation? Crush Israel's foes, the abhorrent gentiles?

Like a gob of gristle stuck in one's craw, a guttural sound burbled up from his neck. No! He laughed. No! He shook his head. No, he knew it, no, and no, and definitely, absolutely not!

If his mother Mary's look upon him had ever tempted Yeshua ben Joseph to think he might be the Messiah, since that Passover when his identity had been presented, he felt his life was for everyone. So, instead of meeting his mother's eyes—Mary always expecting miraculous signs—he took to the hills of Nazareth alone. He climbed that northern hill, once known as a "High place of Baal," and a part of his people's history. From the top he gazed out on Megiddo where the Egyptian army had won victory, and the Judean king met defeat. Mid-distance was Tanakh where Deborah and Barak won out over Sisera. Ahead lay the hills of Dothan where Joseph's brothers sold him into slavery. In the distance lay mounts Gerizim and Ebal with their traditions about Abraham and Jacob. Sitting on the side of this hill, he was turning his people's history over in his mind, trying to see how to unite his energy with their destiny as a race.

But no clear light would come.

A certain day in autumn. The heat and the flies were still horrible when the messenger from Sepphoris charged into the yard. Their father Joseph was working on a palace for Herod Antipas. A derrick had collapsed. Joseph was injured! Yeshua wanted to tear to his father, but Mary, taking their brother James with her, was to be the one.

By the time Mary arrived Joseph had died. His death was as soundless as his life. From Sepphoris they brought his body home. And Joseph was laid to rest with his fathers.

Grief whelmed the house as tight as a net. Mary, awaiting her last infant, was implacable. She wept, and wept. Each child was athwart with loss. So to him as the eldest, the whole of their lot fell. The rearing of his siblings, the shop work and finances, the care of his mother, all this was now his. A least that question of him being a Jewish-Deliverer, or even to respond to the knowledge received in Jerusalem that night, all choice was whisked away, wiped from Yeshua by the death of Joseph.

Life became sheer toil. Iron, leather, wood and metal were his days. He planned, he bartered, he solved and saved. Ruth, the last child, was born. Yeshua became her young brother-father, nursing the baby when Mary slept. At nights he strode about holding the new child against his strength and grief, grief for the loss of their melancholy, wonderful father, Joseph. But she, their Ruth, she was here, here in the world, and here in his arms, this precious new baby life. However sore after work, he played the harp and went on weaving tales for the older children. From his cherished Greek Scriptures he read to them, adding a shout of "Welcome! Come in!" to the neighbors who would pop in to listen at nights. Passing beggars leaned in by the door. At times, there might stroll in a cow, a chicken, and the ass as

## John, Rebecca and the Zealots

well, and they all, James, Miriam, Joseph, Martha, Simon, Jude, Amos, and the baby Ruth, everyone grew closer.

They missed Joseph though. And always would.

At least his "career" was settled. If truth be told, he was relieved. The temple had troubled him. So had the animal sacrifices, the priests' politicizings, their rants about sin and the on-coming apocalypse. He would have bent over backwards to learn from the smallest child—but would have sat at no man's feet to learn how to think about God.

So he worked. Ten to be fed, he hadn't a moment to himself. James was selling the doves for Mary now. They had a second cow, with Miriam virtually the milk merchant of the region. But their money was a squeeze, never enough. Innerly he had been shifting, no longer an open, candid child. His body, never a source of shame or pride, was changing quickly too. Joseph's absence, he felt it, the appalling gonenness of the man. But as the village tattle about him had ebbed he was glad to bury his unsought-for difference back into God. If anything, he was relieved to be even more ordinary, to no longer have to agonize on how and when to begin. When God's hour was come, it would get him ready.

One night, chafed and bleary after work, he was reading a remote passage in the Scriptures. During his study, he found a brief passage from Enoch. It mentioned one of the traditional titles for a teacher, "Son of Man." This figure of Scripture was a messenger, one who spoke of God and was therefore said to be a Son of Man, one entirely at the Father's service. Now this, this at least, it was more like how he felt about himself. No, he didn't experience himself as the "Enlightened One" or as "Jewish Deliverer" but simply, as Enoch said, a Son of Man, born of humanity, a child of mortal kind. Yeshua embraced the title. But he did not speak of it then. How strange, but in these years of waiting he was becoming more and more silent . . .

Of the visit to his mother by an angel he knew nothing, having emptied himself of all superhuman knowing. But now, like any a youth, he was envisioning, creating from his own soul what it lacked. In his vision he saw a person, a friend who helped you get closer to what life was, what others were, walk with you towards who you really are. It wasn't a day-dream, more like imagining someone who knew your purposes, which, he had to admit, had gone hazy by now. Hammering and sawing away at the bench, he went on working alone. He lived one day at a time. He decided because he had to, everything by himself.

Work was steady. But he was earning less. Civil taxes rose. And then so did the Temple tax. He worked from early till late. But he still could not earn enough money for his family. Fearing that the taxman would nab his one treasure, he grabbed it from the shelf. He ran with the Greek Scriptures to the synagogue's library, donating it on his fifteenth birthday. Now it would belong to all Nazareth.

Joseph had worked hard for Herod, literally to his death. A good sum of money was owing their father when he died. The family were counting on it. There was an official hearing. So Yeshua had to attend. Herod Antipas who had survived his own father's massacres, had the sullen, porcine mask of a sneak. As a man with no standards of his own is vulnerable to all excess, so Herod Antipas, knowing nothing, imagined everything. Addicted to paranoia, atrocity and stinginess, Herod ruled that not a shekel was owing to the family of Joseph.

From that time on, the son-of-Joseph half sneeringly called Antipas, "that fox."

By now his family were really poor, even for Nazareth. Their food was meagre. Breakfast was plain bread. It was yeastless and flat, to make it last longer. Nightfall saw the best of their food, corn, the marrow, scant as it was. Rarely, there was a fish. All their lands were sold, gone. But they had vegetables. North of Nazareth, Yeshua rented a stretch of soil with some olive trees on it. Every one of the family, even baby Ruth, still but a chit, had their own plot in it. They grew tomatoes, potatoes, and all the greens. Yeshua worked with the children here. They dug, they sowed, weeded, harvested. Sometimes they spoke of Joseph. At nights they sang, they joked about, ate and washed, and sang again, then prayed to God their thanks. This was their existence, their poor mean days, but entirely good and sufficient.

By his sixteenth year Yeshua's voice had lowered. It had enriched without a crack. And though he paid no heed to such fripperies at all, his voice was to be called by others, "musical." His body was agile, sinewy and deft. His movement was decisive, its assurance natural. And without him knowing it, a distinctiveness rang off him like light off stone. Glamor—in reality, the projection of others—floated about him. And once again people were recognizing a force in him that was surely a destiny. Yeshua of Nazareth, they were whispering again, was to be Israel's Deliverer, well, the Mentor of Galilee, at the very least. But he thought he was for something less clangorous, less material than that. Sure, he was of this world, intrigued by its every mote and fleck, he was tied, body, bone and muscle to it. But the call in him was towards humans, to know them for their own sakes—yes, first always that! —and because of all he had to say to this world of Man, whose Son, their son, he was.

Of course he tried—and how many times! —speaking of this with his mother. Mary sorrowed for him having to work this hard. When it was for glory that her boy had been destined! When he tried to tell her how it really was with him, Mary listened, her face smudged in a smile of unwavering adoration. Her head held at an angle of doting blankness, she listened entranced without hearing a word he said. She would smile blindly, and nod, and nod at her lovable son, and go on stirring the lentils. He tried taking her hand; to make her stop, hear him. But Mary went on nodding, and stitching or shelling. Over and again, she could only repeat the same set-in-stone scenario she had in mind for him from the time of her visitation by that Angel from God. Since then Mary knew her first born was to be their Messiah, savior of their nation, deliverer of glory and bread. So he, the recipient of her augury and fixation couldn't speak to her.

That year Amos, their baby brother, died of fever. The family was staggered by grief. Mary's heart wrecked, his mother stepped back, and Yeshua took over the overseeing of all to be done. At the death of Amos, Mary declined all decision and authority over the house.

It was his seventeenth year. And now real trouble came—the Zealots. And Yeshua, a good Jew really, had to look at it, that party of revolt against Rome. If his people's core passion was to stay separate from others, to detest all foreigners, they had the God of the universe to hold them to that. As the drama of Scripture testified, Yahweh had told "his" people to smite the abhorrent nations. The Eternal One, loving them more than everyone else, was ready to turn all others into footstools under Israel's feet. So said Scripture. And so felt the nation. And the Zealots were but a nuance of this. But when with teeth and rapiers flashing, they barged into the Nazareth house to recruit him, Yeshus, like a good mate, took off his worker's apron and welcomed them anyhow. He sat on a low, three legged stool and listened to what they said. The rest of the family present, Mary waited on these severe politicals with that tucked-away tea from Damascus, offering them her speciality, dainty little sesame cakes. The Zealots declared, "Romans are vermin. The crucifiers of our land. Look at us! The crucified nation! Bled dry by taxes!"

He wanted to say, "Well, it's only money . . . External rule doesn't touch the soul. Rome is only power, husk, the outside!" He wanted to say, power can't get to a thing in you, not the viscera of lives! Nor could it be true, as the Zealots kept yelling, that all Romans were pigs. It chilled him, the race-vanity of these pious assassins who now said it was the patriotic duty of every Jew to kill anything Roman. After the patriots had yelled themselves hoarse, Yeshua tactfully said he was not able to join their plan, his family needing him at home.

"We will supply your family with funds," they flared back.

"Money cannot love," he mildly replied, but knew he was losing ground.

"You can't withdraw like that!" they warned him, "This is not a time for 'love'! Or of the individual!"

But his expression said there was never time for anything but that. They burst at him. They railed. His duty! His nation! His race! Aglow with the cause also, Mary went at him, he, her boy, just sitting there on that low, abject stool. "This is a betrayal, my son. Your refusal to help your nation is disobedience! You are breaking your pledge to us in Jerusalem."

Dreading this, he hardly dared to ask, "W-what pledge?"

"To be obedient to your parents."

His chin fell with shock. All he could say to Mary was, "How could you . . . ?"

Though, as he touched her shoulder, Mary withdrew her claim—for the present. Turning to the Zealots, he didn't know how to conclude without giving offense. Their pointy knives winking on their belts, they let it be known, trouble would follow for his family if he refused. That minute, to be the one when Yeshua began to lose prestige in Nazareth, James, his clever brother, stepped in.

"Hey!" winked James, complicit and chummy with the seething Zealots, "Say you leave Yeshua with us," he creamed on all palsy-walsy, "leave him as our family-father, and instead of one for the cause, he will raise five loyal patriots!" Yeshua's reputation as a young family-father had spread further than Nazareth. And with Jews such a thing was an honor.

The Zealot-crisis was over. For now. But afterwards in Nazareth there was a split of opinion about this "Son-of-Man" youth. He was known for his helpfulness, for his devotion, yes, but not especially to his own. And with much of Nazareth's regard lost, he was never to be quite popular here again.

But then, what exactly did public esteem matter? He was living only for what had early surged in him, then ebbed, and was now rushing again like the ocean at him, the time he could turn fully to others, and himself fully to word and deed.

In his eighteenth year Yeshua went up to the Passover in Jerusalem with James, his brother to be received, as he had been five years ago, into the Commonwealth of Israel. On their way south, Yeshua tried to prepare James for what he might see—droves of animals slain, the blood flung against stone, the priests' hysterical over-emphasis of sin, the bizarre trade in the temple. But James wasn't that shocked. He took a swipe at the heartless Sadducees, the self-precious and bludgeoning style of the priests, and laughed, "Let's look forward to a time when you, my brother, set things right." A balanced, even tempered lad, James had a fine time meeting people. And his older brother did not contend with him. He went quietly with James, being there just for him.

And happiness was Bethany once again. A snaky road of bandits and lizards, it led to their best of friends, to Martha, Mary and Lazarus. From Jerusalem the two Galileans bore the paschal lamb to Bethany, a pleasant village of cypresses, a shady well, ladles of water, the glad munching of food, the hands of friends. Everyone in the household had a wonderful time talking, easy and real with one another. They sat the Passover Seder, ate, prayed, sang, exchanged news, ideas, promises, then left. The two from Nazareth returned to the repair shop. They worked on. Yeshua was meeting the humans of the day and really liking them. Common people told him their saved-up jokes and troubles, then went on their way, heard out, delighted. That year he had a project; to pull together the divergent tracks of his emotions and intellect. It was to learn how to trust the God-Spark within, that censor-of-reality which never permitted anyone to be deceived or brainwashed, or become a helpless victim of one's own sensations, that universal voice of God from within that told you what was true, what was not, and what was what.

His eighteenth year. It was September. Mary's relative from Judea, Elizabeth, came at last to visit with her son John. Over the years, the place of John had been prepared in Yeshua's mind. From report, he had a picture of his cousin in the Judean desert, tending sheep, wearing the skin of an animal. But Yeshua also knew John in the world of vision, his soul waiting, his heart open to heaven, a wild man of God.

The way Elizabeth and Mary greeted one another in the yard in Nazareth, to the children watching, it looked as if the mothers had a pact. In their cries of greetings was the undertow of something known, and long agreed upon. They were women whose husbands had both been reconciled to the birth of their sons by an angel-dream; to Joseph that their infant was to reveal to those who would receive it, that they were God's child; to Zacharias that his wife was to bear the herald of the Soul-Healer. Now Mary and Elizabeth were cooing eagerly, looking dazed from dazzling son to son. But the young men stood at a reserve from one another. John was swarthy, almost ebony, his skin a scorched metal, he looked aflame, his hair out-swept and unkempt. But in him burnt the valor of a great obedience. The way John stood, legs apart and waiting, he seemed given to a purpose beyond himself. Nor was John's purpose an ecstasy of the emotions, but the truth that had appeared in him. What it might be hadn't at all cleared in the wild young Judean. And of late, he had been wondering, would it ever? But he would wait. John's was not some pat expectation of apocalyptic or political ravage, then national salvation and elevation; he had no dreams of the Chosen People's domination, no vainglory, nothing collective. No, he didn't know what he was waiting for. But he was. And would. And if need be, for life. Perhaps the spirit of this waiting had come upon him in his life as a shepherd in the sandy wastes of Judea, a gatherer of honey, eating locusts, ranging the crests and wadis by himself. He might have even said, what he was waiting for was a way, or for a truth. Or, when with a shock John saw him coming forward to him across the yard, for the kind of man his cousin was becoming.

Yeshua, only a little younger, was fairer, more graceful. He was a smiler, and had a focus quite other than John's. Actually, Yeshua laughed a lot, being gentler, more cheery and clearly from the more ethnically mixed Galilean lands. Surveying one another in the yard, both young men were tense. The mothers were hoping they would link up, perhaps become a preaching tandem. But there in the dust of the Nazareth yard, both knew their significance for each other would be far more than that. In front of their egging-on audience the boys said little, nothing beyond a formal embrace.

Later, they found each other. It was evening and they walked out over the hills. Just not touching, but brothers in the same kind of burning together, they strode in the wind, shoulder to shoulder, exchanging their ideas on humanity and the world. Then they were more personal, face to face. "All my life," the dark youth was saying as they lounged against the terse high rocks overlooking Nazareth, "I've despised the shallowness that lets humans prefer their made-up selves to the wholeness of God. I would serve—to the point of blood—whatever it is . . . "

"So, John," in the shade of evening, his kinsman's head was averted, "let's wait..."

When he looked at his cousin, John felt he had been heard. "Are you the one," by then he had heard and seen enough to ask, "for whose life-work I am?"

"Wait, John. We will know when." His cousin smiled that light, surrendered smile, and when they parted, both promised to wait. They agreed to not break their silence until the Lord's hour, knowing themselves part of each other's fate. Without any more words, in the morning John left. He would care for his elderly mother, tend sheep outside Hebron in Judea, turning those to God who would, and wait.

Some years ago, after Joseph's death, Yeshua had written on a smooth board of Lebanese cedar a prayer for everyday people. "Our Father," it began. More and more people saw it, asked if they could have it, and wrote it down too. In the village he was being gradually known as the God-turned one, a Son of Man. But in that credulous world of prophets and miracles, if he was to be a teacher of truth, why had he not chosen a more prestigious title like, "Messenger of God"? Or, even "Immanuel"?

No! He recoiled. His message was not to out-do those of others. Nor would it be magical or mystical. What he had to say to humans was in friendship, hardly to political groups, but to the individual. So, he thought, yes, "Son of Man," he would stick with that image of Enoch's. Because his word to humans would be like a son's, that's how he felt, like a son to all.

He woke early, worked late, laboring all the time. Money was not nothing to him, but a tangible measure for effort. He respected money as a means, securing education for his sisters and brothers. For, weren't they now his children? And weren't they a lovely bunch? Their young brother Joseph was cheery, though a plodder, Simon a dreamer but sweet, Jude was a hot-head, James ever smart and refined, Miriam a prudent beauty with a fine intellect, Martha slow, but you could bet your life on her. And Ruth, their last, she was very funny, a spontaneous sunshine. Since Mary had bowed-out to Yeshua's management, all home-decisions were his. In those times there were no schools for girls; they were not supposed to use their intellect. Well, he seriously resented this! So he devised a home-school with the older ones teaching the younger. After the days' labor he taught them himself, Miriam, Martha, Ruth. Against their own grumblings he insisted they learn letters, numbers, history and about the philosophies of God. He taught them at night and listened to them. He posed problems, heard out their answers. If the village had once imagined Yeshua ben Joseph as a renowned scholar at the elite academies of Jerusalem, it was now certain to him, it wasn't going to happen. Actually, he couldn't have studied with the hereditary priests and scribes, both castes fuming with mutual hate. But he gladly learnt from his sisters, from any child, from the way of a dog, or duck, or the scary scorpion, even from a leaf's striations. He was glad too to have no time to indulge in self-analysis or mystic self-reflections.

Enough that there was growing in him a complex accumulation of his otherwise unutterable pre-existence, a process so uncharted that it locked him not into secrecy but into a muteness about itself.

There were times though when it would clear in him, that undivided purpose for which he lived: to reveal to those who wanted it, and would hear of it, the love of the Father for all.

But how? With what act? Or word? And, exactly when?

If by nineteen, you asked him, "How do you fare?" he would have replied he was much loved by his family but because of entrenched mindsets nearly always misunderstood by them. He would have said, he had organized some of his many impulses, if not yet to readiness, enough to first do the necessary, rear his dear ones, see them marry, set out for life. Nor would he tell you with a helpless smile, would he be the Jewish Messiah. Though some people, like his mother still dreamt he was. He was a Jew, yes, but for all that it meant, his mission was humanity. And Heaven's will might be no more for him than to be a witness to the truth in silence.

Then was it in the history of his fate that he had to consider her—Rebecca.

She was a gorgeous maiden, a single, thick and gleaming plait down her back. Daughter of a prosperous merchant in Nazareth, she was a clear-minded girl, given to no female snits or the usual coquettishness. Nor did she flaunt her obvious virtues like her adorable plumpness, or how she could turn out an eye-rollingly delicious sesame cake, or those things she was really very good at, like light bouts of social sparring, or winning at serious debate with young men. She knew how to see things, and to say them, but because of innate refinement held back from using her advantages. There was a violence of focus, and of a restraint that passed for passion in Rebecca, and men would be drawn to her for it in later life, mistaking it for the power of the erotic—but it wasn't, no, not at all.

## John, Rebecca and the Zealots

The whole thing began at the young people's gatherings in Nazareth. The young group of philosophizers were a meteoric lot. They discussed gentile religions, Chinese music, Hellenic ideas, the Arabic tribes and lands. And most radically, even for the Galil, all classes of people, even girls were welcome to be present. This day, Rebecca had taken part in the group's debate on the mystical versus the rational way to God. Concluding her point in an irrefutable flourish, she swung her plait with a snap, and turned to sit down. She was shrugging even, couldn't care less about her win, and bent sideways a little to sit down on the bench. When, from a corner of her eye she saw him, Yeshua ben Joseph. Not a theatrical girl, her breath caught. He was just turning his head to listen to a friend's remark in that sunny way he had, when Rebecca, chancing to glimpse the life in him, the ease of that unbelievable masculine beauty he had, looked away, turned red with unspecified desire, and fell silent. She didn't look again. Or, not soon. For a while she held it there—an explosion of diamonds in her head. But the next time she looked across her friends to him, Rebecca lowered her head. Change, she knew, was on the way. What had happened was ecstasy. But her own emotion not the source of it, she knew it was from the Source of reality itself. For the instant of her seeing him, her life mounted on a wave of shock and stayed peaked in the surge, caught, frozen.

She did not gulp, blush, or rush it, just looked at him calm, no girlish sauciness—he was used to that—a fortunate ancestry and rigorous physical labor having made of him what was generally admitted to be a splendid specimen. Over the months Rebecca let it happen. When in their group, she made herself blank to simply listen to the content of what the young man Yeshua said. She watched him say it, took it in, let it rush into her, a burst of absolute truth. When she heard his words about God and Man, she felt brought to reality's core. From then she knew, he was right, just perfectly so, the loveliest of men. She longed for him, though not really for him to be hers, but in a way she didn't then know what it meant. How does a longing for love to be inclusive of all—of mood, touch, senses and sex, the uniqueness of a person—how does a love like that ever meet its answer? Rebecca loved Yeshua ben Joseph as a man, no question of it. She loved what lived in him, the unworked authority of it. She loved his way with others, the way he was with children, how, when he spoke he made nothing of himself and much, very much of everyone else. The times she heard him talk with people, as tenderly as God might with a small child, Rebecca was stung, a bit jealous, but knew; such tenderness could never belong only to her! At love's depth she lost all shyness in the suffering of it. Though, even before going after him, she knew there was a set-apartness in him, a destiny tremendous, tragic, and terrible. For what he was had been an arrangement from reality and not some vain role he had made up for himself. He was reserved for something; she knew it from what lived in his eyes. And it was intrinsic and shattering.

Nevertheless, she tried. But first, she told Miriam. And his sister told Mary. And they both went to Rebecca who repeated her story to them.

His mother Mary, on hearing Rebecca's stumbling confession, looked at the girl with the face of one being slapped. "To lose the chief bread-winner of the family!" was Mary's first reaction.

"My father will support you all," Rebecca assured her. "Like a son, he already loves Yeshua!'

"So," responded Mary, "does everyone." Miriam beside her, Mary told the girl of their belief that Yeshua was a son of destiny. He was to be a leader. And a great one. Even perhaps, Mary warned Rebecca, the Messiah.

All the more flamed Rebecca's love. Securing the consent of her father, she invited Yeshua to their home. Her father, as patriarch, spoke generally at first. Then he mentioned marriage to the deeply listening young man. But when Yeshua spoke up, it was to say he was first to rear his own family, the most sacred of trusts. Rebecca's father stood up. He walked out, muttering to his child, "We can't have him, too noble for us." But he left the two alone.

Rebecca turned to him. "Yeshus," she smiled, and with a level voice of no emphasis whatever said she loved him, had loved him for ages, and she would. And forever.

His eyebrows shot up. She had moved him beyond words. He had never looked the force of human passion in the eye, its nobility, the force of nature in it, and the depth. Nor had he ever been this helpless. Rebecca was a girl favored and high in every sense. But he had not thought of marriage. True, he knew the body's stirrings towards sex, and though strong, it was not attached to anyone in particular. He did long for intimacy, the urge to unite, but the energy of love going out to everyone, it left him free. Or because his life was already caught up elsewhere, sexual desire never became particular to any person in him. Giving his love to the one person would have focused it, but also limited it, instead of the world-spread for which he felt his energy was meant. How to explain this to Rebecca? Or, for that matter, fully to himself? How to say it, sexual union was a pure good in itself, even ideal, but then, as an intensification of self in the mutuality that absorbed you, it was also a closing out of others. Since that Jerusalem event, his life was being wrestled into complete self-forgetfulness, his nature being eclipsed by a force of divinity dawning through him. How to say this, any of it, to her?

They stood in the room together. She, soft plaited before him, as beautiful as anything really loved and beheld. Though there was no bar to her becoming his private woman for the satisfaction of emotion and sex, such compromises of private nature and public role did not exist for them. Not in him, nor in Rebecca. For unified people, desiring wholeness in sex, the personal life of a man and a woman side by side and the children it made went naturally together.

"Rebecca" . . . he said to her, his face broken to its most tender, "that you once loved me shall always cheer me," he wasn't sure how to go on, but did. "But I don't yet know what is to be. If something is to come from me, then," he pointed to the Galilee world now sumptuous in the summer outside, "how . . . ?" He couldn't complete this, not knowing his own thought.

But she did. She already knew. Her face did not move. What failed in her that moment was beyond the saying of it. And far from exploding, or crumpling, her expression stayed set. Hadn't she always known he would be a man of uncompromising honor, that marriage and its creative condition naturally including children would be inseparable for him. So then, on hearing the inevitable, Rebecca only said, "Yes, I know," and looked away with a smile of entire acquiescence that was genuine.

Still, it broke her.

But she understood. Soon she was even able to go on. And really so. Rebecca didn't even mind the loss of all sexual desire from then, the loss of need for self-expression in intimate and exclusive possession, because after all, hadn't she consented to everything in advance because of him?

Afterwards, of course she begged her father to move to Sepphoris, a town away from Nazareth.

"But my dear," her perplexed dad said, "there is no shame on you! We don't have to move for you, you know."

"O, No! Not me!" her fine eyebrows arched mildly surprised as she laughed.

"For *him*!"

*Chapter IV*

# A Pilgrim

He was human, this much he knew. He slept, he hungered, he felt low, he soared, he sorrowed, he dreamt. Like any sane man, he had a drive to know what was real. At the same time, he felt threaded through by the inexplicable, the divine. Finding the intersection of divinity with the animal in him was his first task. But he would have to grow to it, to know what it was. Life was going to be as hard as that; if he did his task, he would know his role. When he began to do it, he would know who he was.

There was, as always, a short-cut. With a little illicit maneuver of mind he could have snatched it, just wrenched the answer from his own imagination. But he had renounced all the tricky accesses to self. Besides, since that hailing under the stars in Jerusalem, there was a clear life of speaking, a word yearning out of him. The gist of that word was simple, evident to good will and sense; that everyone came from, and was going to, God. It was the order of creation, and everyone was a part of it. This was the kingdom, no items of exclusion, everyone belonged. This was his message; it was *always* the message, even if its public hour had not yet come. While your own personal moment of living the Father was always now.

Hard work kept him grounded. Handling iron, canvas and stone, he was learning. Matter was obdurate; it made severe incursions on a man. However toughened by labor, he experienced that exhaustion when every atom in your arms and back hurt and you just want to lie down in the dust. He knew the spin in the head when all nutrition ran out of the blood, the reeling, self-evaporating feel of hunger, the scour of thirst, the mad-making

*A Pilgrim*

craving of it. Hammering and fitting, sawing away at the work bench, he kept his spirit drive alive, always minding how to hold it together with a sharp sense of other humans. Whatever the stress, he was sure you could live the life of heaven right here, here on this rough but adequate earth. Most daring of all was listening to the Father's intent breathing in yourself. Still harder to follow it. To trust the guidance you are being given, do it in faith, and without presumption.

True, sometimes he was confused. Then he doubted much of this. Of only his humanity was he certain. The rest of his self-understanding was staggered, patchy, many loose ends. He had no signs, no nudges from the universe, no prods or winks from events. Only one thing had ever happened to him outside nature—that by now hazy injunction in Jerusalem, to be about the Father's business.

As an intellectually scrupulous Jew, he had to sort this one—had it been just an invention? His own mind chattering to itself? Because, if you segmented reality down to its last material and logical degree, that Jerusalem proposition to him could not be understood outside the framework of madness.

So, was he mad?

But the question ruled itself out.

Nevertheless, there remained some very serious gaps in the working of his mind on this. He drove at it; was his vocation from God? Or was the urge to speak to humans about God just an obsession? Because if this was an idea he had made up for himself, then he was a fool, and would be immolated on the pyre of his own vanity for it. But if it were true . . . and he shuddered at the abyss of necessity opening in him at that. So he stayed with the question. No, he wouldn't just snooze on it or snap it shut in a blind assertion. Only years later would he see it didn't matter if the Father chose you or you offered yourself. Any unmixed love for the Source of Reality in a human was a consecration to which the arms of Heaven opened.

Anyway, he decided to not agonize over his identity, busy as he was with the living of it.

Poverty. His family really was poor. They were always needing more and more bread. Sandals too. A saddle for the ass. A separator of milk and cream. Chalk, and reams of papyrus for his young ones to practice writing. Seeds for the garden. A cloak for young Ruth. The daily grind was endless. Their ages now ranging from seven to seventeen, he was kept on his toes listening to their high-pitched emotional lives. His family, what an expressive lot! How they talked! They talked and talked, they talked their heads off long into each night. Simon had graduated that year from school and to start work with Yeshua's friend, Jacob, by now a stone mason. Soon, he was to take Joseph, a freckly lad with a voice of gently meandering diction, to Jerusalem. James had become a crisp young man, his talk brisk, his shoulders square, his eye vigorous. Miriam was known in the region as a vendor of best yoghurt and dealer in cheese, as well as the unrivalled beauty of Nazareth. Martha was still a plump shy girl who kept her counsel, stuck to the given, and wove exquisite cloth. Jude was short-fused, explosive as a Chinese cracker. And Ruth, unfolding, was no longer a baby. His mother, once a-brim with ambition, was a quieter woman. Mary, whose aspirations had once soared for him, now seemed subdued. She was still a busy grower of herbs, a hearty natured woman, but her smile at times seemed, if not lost, almost ineffable. He, her son, felt his mother's sadness, but knew; no mechanism existed in the entire universe to will his mother's fantasies into a reality they did not possess. The instant a desire achieved consistency with the universe, it would achieve due form. Mary's tragedy was that, with the best of will and heart, she was unable to conform her mind to what was.

Money matters ran to the ground. His family needing more of everything and with James still to be run-in as their alternate family head, Yeshua decided, and not easily, he would work a while in the gentile city of Sepphoris.

"Oh why! Why?" grizzled his variously disgruntled brood, sensing a larger preparation behind this venture.

"Just in case," Yeshua fluffed the hair of "his kids," as they clownishly called themselves.

Indeed, with several other aims in mind, he arranged to train with a smith in Sepphoris. Walking his lightly packed beast into the din of merchants, hucksters and prostitutes hawking their wares, he felt like a naive Jew from provincial Nazareth. Moving through the city's beat, oppressed by the sight of women touting themselves, the hawkers swindling everyone less from greed than habit, he wrestled with the clearing, if uncomfortably stupendous, sense of being somehow a part Creator of all this.

A human intersected by Creator-divinity did not feel sublime to him, more like a cyclone. He endured it by disciplining himself to it. He gave it no expression as he trudged lugging his bag of scant belongings, mildly leading the scruffy donkey, stepping over the humid hummocks of the dear beast's droppings. It wasn't easy, this being wedged between divinity and humanity. He suffered the in-rush of the Absolute into this dimension, the hardly endurable strangeness of it. A hurricane of universes beating through him, he trod the ruts and cobbles of Sepphoris with the look of a man walking through a vortex.

How was he not atomized by it?

He kept his eyes down, down on the road, and his mind on God. Whether hammering at the forge as he trained with the smith, or tethering to shoe a pack animal with the formations and histories of entire galaxies barrelling in his consciousness, Yeshua survived by keeping his mind's-eye on the ground, on the ground of himself, and on this earth. As this, the cosmos of his own making manifested to him in a vertical descent of information, it pierced the horizontal plane of his peaceful human consciousness. But he kept himself still in it, a virtual crucifixion, kept himself here, quiet, and open to the Father of it. He could bear the anguish of a universe because he kept himself small, and even in the ecstasy of all possibility, faced to his Father God.

Otherwise, even he, a being of the highest order, might have not endured it.

Also, he endured the in-rush of the cosmos, amounting to the real crucifixion of the man, to prove a human was endued imbued with enough of divinity to withstand the assault of all the worlds. His simple act of staying anchored to God proved it, this is what humans have, that a consciousness fixed to the one point was enough to absorb and move above a whole universe.

While in Sepphoris, he had also to face it, the reason he left Nazareth. It was to wean his family from emotional dependence on his presence. Living away from them hurt him as well. Still young himself, he needed closeness, the physical contact. He also desired what very few Jews did at the time, to learn the workings of the gentile mind. Since that Passover week in Jerusalem when he had met scores of young people from the globe's Far East and West, he had a deep wish to travel. There was a journey in him; actually, there were several. Journey, as an act of passage was essential to what he was to say. He wanted to learn the soul-natures of the planet. But he would wait. In Sepphoris he was gearing himself in the self-support skills, becoming adept at several, in particular, the forge and anvil.

Still, were he to be frank about it, half a year later when James had so well proved himself as domestic head, Yeshua heaved a sigh of relief to be returning home. He had missed, really and sorely, badly missed his chirpy brood. Just to hold again his brothers and sisters in a bunch-hug, or singly, each in his arms! Still young, he craved the familiar, the affectionate home habit. And he had missed the caravan shop where he was of use, a fixer and solver of everything.

Once home again, he was living his days in a deep mood of thanks. At day's end of work, he might look over the hacked and oily benches. Or stare out to that roan red color of the land and feel the tides of sheerest peace floating off the hills of Nazareth. How glad was he once more to be inside the golden whorl of the Galil's autumn, its fruity airs with the cranes and mallards, the swifts and the grouse, and always, of course, the sempiternal sparrows, each of whom he was sure were known to God. In these rolling Galilee days he was being granted a respite. So he worked on, hard and glad and in quiet for a precious little time more.

He grew into the manhood of a robust and refined man. Those of lofty mind might play this down, but the physicality of Yeshua ben Joseph was visually superb. He was a strong, a well-set and muscular carpenter, his energy of movement an animal grace, his gold-brown colors quietly startling, his looks prodigiously good. A modest, and in no way a silly man, he thought himself fortunate to be living in a strict Jewish context where such things were of not much account. But not so with the intellect. In the Hebrews' religious world the mind was valued for what it reflected of God. And by now he was being requested to teach at Nazareth's synagogue. As he was getting to know, so was he letting himself be known by many people, who, hearing him in synagogue carried report of him as a man of first magnitude abroad.

In his twenty-third year Yeshua took Simon to Jerusalem for his brother's entry into community as a Son of the Covenant. Alien to the politics of it, young Simon was spellbound by the grandeur of the temple. His older brother stood by, not saying a word. Personally, the temple still worried him. Its priests were a hereditary caste of ritual slaughterers, a hierarchy of panderers —frauds to be exact! They taught atonement by sacrifice, their insistence on sin a justification of their parasitic existence. For Simon's sake, Yeshua gagged his fury at their obscene teachings about God's wrath—what an affront to the Father! —imagining to buy his favor by the shedding of innocent blood! He was never at ease in this city of wranglings and excludings, of vile butchery and breast-thumping, spit-flying disputations.

That year in Jerusalem Yeshua met the greatest of his early temptations. It materialized through a goodly merchant of Damascus. A well educated traveller, this Damascene wanted to establish a school of religious philosophy. He had heard tell on the caravan circuits of Nazareth's remarkable speaker. When the merchant met him, he was so impressed—what a *doing* this Jew had in him! —that he invited the young rabbi to be the head of his college in Damascus. The proposed teacher-to-be had to seriously consider it. Firstly, he would have a life of public voice, a platform of significance. Fame would accrue to him. It would give him the leverage to speak of the one thing he absolutely desired to, the reality of God's love. At the possibility of such an opportunity, he was torn. Here it was! The chance to do the work for which he lived. Was this the path to it?

He refused the spectacular career. And with it, he declined the power of a teacher placed at a pivot of influence. A prestigious platform would have falsely authorized what he was to do, exactly what he didn't want! Fame would have made his person too prominent. The position would have eclipsed the teaching. And he never wanted to speak from a throne, nor by the authority of any institution of respect. His words were to come more from the roadside, or from the shores of any sea, from the by-ways or the hillsides to Man. For were he to prop his authority with external proofs, where would be the self-discovery for his hearers? Where their personal assent? Where their own decision for faith? To bring God's help to people was one aim of his. To kindle pure faith was another. But neither faith nor works would mean a thing if they came by means of prestige or power. Everything he was to do would be misunderstood outside faith and love.

Also, what was the point of speaking about God to those already favored, full of ideas, the able, the rich, scholars, the comfortable-minded and lettered? No, he wanted to speak to the poor of spirit, to the hapless, to those on the edge. His word was firstly to be for those who had nothing, those who didn't know, those poor in opinion, the unsure.

So he let the glory go.

After this salubrious offer of a career triumph from the world he returned to Nazareth and lapsed into obscurity again.

The years of his twenties were all a leave-taking from all the legitimate comforts of home and landscape and friends. The most painful of farewells was from his family. He knew each one very well, loved them all with a natural blood-bond affection, as well as each for the person they were. But what he was called to do was narrowing to a point and about to ask of him everything comfortable, pleasing, and right. He would have to give it all, even to go into the roads of the world, away from roof and hearth, away from everything he now knew defined him.

So, he was getting ready. A fast was being prepared for his family. And a fast for himself as well. They loved him so. And he loved them. But in a way he couldn't describe to anyone, and hardly to himself, he belonged out there, to everyone in the whole world.

In his twenty-fourth year, messengers from Alexandria had sought him out to ask; might he, the well-reputed Galilean, meet them in Caesarea by the sea?

Surprising everyone, he went. The Alexandrian deputation offered him the position of assistant *chazzan* in their illustrious home city. Again the chance of acclaim lay open for the taking. He could have it all, honor, achievement, prestige, éclat. But how to reconcile these with what he was to unfold—the nature of each person's connection to God? So again, and not without difficulty at giving up a good thing, he humbly thanked the Alexandrines very much, and said, "No."

To Nazareth's scowling astonishment, he, to their minds now virtually an Alexandrian philosopher-magnifico, returned to the drudge of menial work. He was coming and going in Nazareth again like any other man. Perhaps he was more public-minded than others. He taught at evening school, he paid mind to everyone, especially to the children. He read in synagogue, spent time with his mother in long chats. To everyone he met he seemed to have the acuteness and refinement of the educated, but it was the untaught deftness of a man in continuous contact with other humans. The sense about him was of a man wielding a huge range of personal force, its restraint adding to its drawing power. He was busy doing for his siblings now. For marriages were in the air. There was Miriam's to his great friend, Jacob, and the wedding of James to Esther. Later were to come the espousals of Joseph and then of Simon. Also, in the shop he was being jostled by the children who came there every day. The smallest of tots would badger him to come play in the sandbox he had hammered together for them. They trundled him out of the shop, tugging his hands, to come, come on, come outside, he, their funny, whimsical man, full of tricks and roars and puns. On a favorite block of stone he would sit spinning stories of the bob-tailed gnu, the jumpy ibexes, the reticulating lizards, and the naked aardvark so ugly he was beautiful, making them laugh.

But when Yeshua prayed, he went alone, alone to nature, always solitary. He went alone, though not to flee, but to find humans, find them more

*A Pilgrim*

truly in his prayer. He would walk over Nazareth's peaty ground, past the valley's thin stand of palms, looking, as he prayed, out on a vista of soft, blanket-textured folds of earth.

Otherwise, the journey was newly pressing him, a voyage to the faraway humans of the world.

After a long stretch of carpentry work, on a rainy morning of a late winter. Yeshua ben Joseph left his home of Nazareth. Putting it vaguely, he said he was going to visit the cities about the Sea of Galilee.

Many times before had he been to the Great Lake. But never had he seen it the way he was about to now, when he walked from Nazareth the entire day to it. From where he stood on the edge of the plane, you could see the lake was a colossal volcano's crater. In that cup of land he saw an aqua jewel, the Sea. That body of water was ringed by a dust pink land rolling back and up from it into a velvet mist. When closer, the sea was a giant pearl with the rainbow playing on its face. Seeing all this, he sat on the ground and gave thanks to God, thanked God to be himself, thanked God to be seeing this, to sit in this land of hills and lilies, poppies, lupines and the iris. On the plain above the Sea he sat, unlikely fields of puce cyclamen encircling him. From the grassy slope where he was eating the flat bread from his swag, he saw spread around him a paradise of herbs and flowers, and he had a sense of vagueness here, a floatation in a glory above the world. If the land of Israel were a metaphor of the Lord's meanings to the Hebrews, then this small Sea of Galilee might be an illustration of his. The land caught the substance of his thought. Its ground contained his message. These things of nature were the flesh of the words he had, these fields and vines, the briers and birds, a mustard seed grown to nearly the size of a chrome bright tree. These meditative pure things of nature held his meanings, being so made as to point to God.

He got up. And went on down. After an hour he was in Tiberius, Herod's new capital. Not much grabbed by that hot, hectic place, a holiday spa for the Emperor Tiberius whose building projects had cost his Joseph father's life, he repaired to Magdala. Nothing much there, a few tawdry businesses, a scatter of crumbly shacks, and he went onto Bethsaida towards the northern neck of the Lake. Where the slopes slid headlong into the sea were the citrus plantations of Capernaum. Chorazin was somewhere in the hills to the side. Gedara of the silent, introverted olives was a village above the sea. On the hills were the small dots of hamlets. Brooks of freshwater brimmed up from the earth sending colorful rills across the early flowering plane. He looked up high to the snow lands of Safed, a town of mystics and magicians. In a single hour the shepherds of Safed could graduate their sheep down to the shore lands already lolling with spring cucumbers and the fat, delicious melons.

Again terribly hungry at the sight of the beauty he ate the last of his mother's stretchy white bread. Opposite from where he sat was the high and freezing Golan, the Shem Jaulan where Job of Uz was born. That side of the Lake was a wind-lashed tundra of destructive fires and hurricanes from the desert, a land boggy, rough and black. From the heights of the Golan plunged ravines, favorite resorts of hyenas and leopards. To the east gleamed the Decapolis cities, quartz-like in the sun. From the mountains the Jordan crashed down cataracts to wind about, dopey on the Hullah, more eccentric than a snake. Due north, scintillate with snow, the white ramparts of Mount Hermon.

By nightfall he was tramping on to the busy town of Capernaum. A little way from it, he found what he sought, the boat shop of Zebedee. His father Joseph's time-sworn friend. Old man Zebedee received Yeshua, Joseph's boy, with the roars and back-thumps of paternal delight. For more than a year Zebedee was to home him with unstinted pleasure. The daughters and sons of the house looked on amazed as this carpenter chap from Nazareth just walked into their compound whistling, and joined their patriarch to become an expert builder of the region's boats. The new partners were a fit, a team. Both men relished tough physical labor. They tried out new techniques, steaming the boards, mixing the lacquers, fiddling with new designs. The superior boats they built drew a superior clientele. In the next five years nearly every vessel on the ancient "Chinnereth" Sea of the Galil could be said to have passed through the hands of these two men.

Yeshua found a home in Capernaum. He was known here as "Yeshus," a maker of boats, a fisherman of grit. He was liked for the salty sting of his wit, the gaiety and humor in that sharp-eyed smile of his. His huge energy still held in reserve, he wanted no note, no attention, his person not to be the issue. He wanted it though for what he was to say about God. And he was. For he was beginning to say it to people, casually and personally, and anywhere it was right, "God is here. God cares. He is coming, and to each, to everyone." He was saying to the people, "God heals you, he makes you whole, God is in every moment of your life, if you will let it be, and turn to him with love."

## A Pilgrim

The day he came out from between those hills, to the folk on the shore who heard him, it was like the miracle of a bird taking wing into the air. In a world of lack, of continuous threat, of grudge, and hunger and ugliness, that a man spoke of love at all was a miracle. That in a world of rage and hopelessness God was your Father was the best news that people had heard in their lives. To their ear it was the truest, the most likely, and personally the best. And on hearing it they found this was what they themselves had always believed as well.

So he was speaking at last, saying it in the streets, on a jetty, a boat, in the hills, under a tree's shade. But he spoke only to individuals. He wanted no mobs. No hordes, no fans. He repulsed all sycophancy, he tolerated no slavishness. Throngs and clamor exhausted him. A man of grave gentleness, he was becoming known in these parts as a "Son of Man." And since hearing him at Capernaum's synagogue, many were calling him, without once being bidden, or him ever asking for it, "Lord," that title of respect, and, though rather young for it, even "Master."

Capernaum had a synagogue of marble, its hue, the shades of a rose. Yeshua was often asked to lead its services. At the Zebedee workshop he was friends with James and John. David was the oldest Zebedee brother and a self-styled atheist, 'Thank God!" he'd laugh, and tell people he was bored by the bellyaching of religion. Well, that was all right; Yeshus and Dov were fast friends. James and John would hold forth their proud ideals on the fruit-shaped hills above Capernaum, while Yeshua spoke of social issues, and, the brothers noted, with no finality. As often, after the day's work, he, a devout Jew, would study Scripture. One night he would meet with the district's older people, with the younger ones on the next. Often present, the Zebedees saw him ask people about their lives, then listen deeply with no other aim than to hear how it was with them. He organized talks. Nearly everyone of the household came. And without remark, he included girls, also the hum-drum matrons who no one took seriously, the unvalued older women, and the frowsy servant helpers on the shore. He took it as given that the least educated also had ideas about life which were crucial to them. These gatherings were his favorite of settled times, their exchange of inquiry, argument, laughs. And then there were the prayers for which they met, the simplest of words said together to God among the deep purple lupines of Galilee's superior green hillsides.

In his twenty-eighth year Yeshua went up to Jerusalem alone. How he relished here the milling of races, Medes, Parthians, Assyrians. But the local

Jews cast slaughterous looks at the foreigners. He had once more to see it; his own people lived in a hatred of strangers. Ethnomania raged. The "Chosen People" conceit was a fantasy of the thwarted about God's attitude to them. To justify it, they locked themselves into a self-concocted ceremonial system, and anyone outside the self-apotheosizing prison of "The Chosen" was a "Son of Darkness," or better still, "the Devil."

And now in the courts of Jerusalem's temple, he, this upstart from the Galil, was talking to his brethren. He spoke of a God turned to all the creation with compassion. Of a God who was a Father, to whom a sinner, a leper, and even a whore was his child. To the Jews who defined themselves against others, what he was saying was past impudence! Their pride of divine election had found in him its worst enemy. He saw nothing sacred in lineage, cared nothing for blood, nought for nation or race. He was saying, be yourself, a child of Heaven; this was all that mattered. Nothing else did. He had a religion about soul; theirs was about their own history, their story, their group, their race, their blood and their fate. The establishment had never heard even a prophet annul your identity, your rank, your status and place. He was a catastrophe, this man. Not that he was attacking the Law. No, there was no attack. He attacked nobody's creed. He tangled with no one's belief. It was where he was pointing, beyond Sin, beyond Guilt, beyond the Law to where the most entrenched of Jewish meanings withered. This man was changing the meanings of words like "sin," and "debt," and "kingdom" and "Father," of "good" itself! So when Jerusalem's authorities heard Yeshua of Nazareth, they knew it: after him everything would change. He would re-structure the soul in anyone who did not shut themselves to it.

So they did. They shut themselves in. They had to.

It was either him or them.

Jerusalem was a cauldron. Everybody hated each other. All the sects, the Zealots, Herodians, Sadducees, always at each other's throats. It was a real dog-fight of sneering, protesting, stone-walling, each caste down-staring the other. As for him! That Yeshua! From pagan Galilee, and from that wretched nothing-good-to-come-out-of-it Nazareth to add! He, he was an affront to all. They despised his unusual meekness, saw it as submission, his putting up with tyranny, his hardly even marking sin. And that "turn the other cheek"? Why, what else was that, but treachery! Even, perhaps, a sly complicity with Caesar! As for dignity, he had none. He behaved as if nothing really felt to him like a slap. But most unsettling of all, that enthusiasm of his! Even when no one applauded it, his energy was unstopped. His word didn't waver because of attack. He never pitched a word for approval. Desiring no allies to prove him right, he stayed on his mettle, sufficient and exact. But the really execrable thing, and the establishment was to get him for it, was his mixing with the all-sorts of Jerusalem, with the yellows, the schwartzs, with women, lepers, fornicators and thieves, all outside the religious 'erub, and by definition, unfit.

And when he heard the word "unfit!" against their brethren, he roared at them, "But God is their Father also!" Many a Jew of that Jerusalem's day stared at him, not so much hostile, as just blank. They knew the Lord God of Israel, they knew the Lord of armies and hosts, but who was this "Father" who caused this Jew (in some ways, such a good one) to defile himself with strangers? Who, they inquired, was this Jew's "Father" on whom, he said all his behavior was based? His sayings were a scandal. His doings were an offense. For a Jew of the Covenant to eat and drink with a pack of vagrants was to stand decency on its head. His buying of vile food from the uncircumcised, then eating it in their company, proved him a deviant, a flouter of the Law.

Yet quite a handful among Jerusalem's pious remembered what the prophets since Leviticus had roared at Israel's heart, "Include in your love the stranger." The charity in him, they saw was supreme, his words were the flower of Israel's true piety, its fruit and only future.

But there were others who remarked, "If this fellow imagines God is his Father, then, who the hell does he think *he* is? Maybe even the Son of Ha Shem?"

"Well, well," the mild older Jews shook their beards with sorrow at the folly and the madness of that, "the penalty for blasphemy could sometimes be really terrible . . . "

Present among Jerusalem's throngs was a father and a son from India. Gonod, a successful merchant, introduced himself to Yeshua. He was about to launch out on a tour, a business odyssey of the Levant. Ganid his son, was a strapping livewire of a boy, he was chafing to hear, see, live. The three of them liked each other so well, that the Indians asked the Hebrew Yeshua to travel with them as Ganid's tutor for the following few years.

In their dusky, cheerful, oriental faces, the invitation to journey opened again. Travel for him would be a quest, a delving into humanity, divinity, and their synthesis. In the Indians' charm of manner, he saw humanity's diversity. He intensely desired to know women and men, their thoughts and culture and personal ways. Through travel he was to meet the high and the low, rich and poor, the animalistic, the mediocre, the exceptional, those who yearned, and those who did not. He would learn from each and give to anyone whatever it was that he had. He desired to communicate, though not yet publicly. He was not entirely possessed of his own purpose or nature, nor had he fully aligned with the spirit, which by now he knew was leading him.

If one value of travel is that it can be a meditation over geographies and history on the nature of Man, Yeshua would seek to learn from it the experience of humanity as lived in this world. From passing through climates, histories and lands, he would learn the condition of humans, what it was to live in time and space.

A few days later their huge ship pulled out from the scruff and sludge of Joppa's shore. As it moved out to open sea, Yeshua felt the burst of adventure push into his veins. Life was the thing, he felt. Life was movement, change, a coming to things, to others, and not only for yourself. He was not out travelling to get *his* own experiences of a private sort to be fondled and hogged to oneself. No, his journey was a pilgrim's voyage, to do it for God as a Man, to live this life, just as he was, living the life he had. No more than that.

The one thing he desired as he entered voyage, was for others to know, God does not want you to be what you are not, but to live this great blessing of life just as you are, just as you have been made.

*Chapter V*

# On the Road

It was April, spring.
    He was leaving Palestine. His companions were Gonod, a man well stropped by the thrust and tussle of Indian merchant life, and his son, aglow with a passion to live, seventeen year old Ganid. Their route to be was, first, the port of Joppa, then up to Caesarea, and out from Palestine across the sea to Alexandria, Crete and Cyrene and onto Carthage. From the African continent they would cross to Malta by boat and onto Sicily's ports of Syracuse and Messina. They would ride and walk up on the Appian Way past Naples to the Latin center of the world, Rome. From there would be a jaunt as far North as what is now Switzerland, back to Tarentum, and by sail to Corinth, Nicopolis, and onto Athens. From Ephesus they would sail to Rhodes and Cyprus, visiting Paphos, Salamis, and back to the Near East's Antioch, Syria. From Sidon they would go to Damascus and by caravan to far Mesopotamia spending time in Babylon, Ur and Susa. After two years of travelling the wanderers three were to stand by the port of Charax, from the sea a vessel approaching to take Ganid and his father back to India.
    His passage across these civilizations was to be a sacred travel. His contact with the individuals met was to be the purest human thrill of Yeshua's life. The Mediterranean was largely under Latin rule, many peopled, loosely universalist. From here would he receive the name by which his mission would be known. From that world, the first to count him as its own and the first to take the Jew, Yeshua ben Joseph to its heart, would come the occidental name of "Jesus."

## His Real Life

Adept at languages, he was to interpret for Gonod by day and teach young Ganid by night. But many hours of adventure were left for himself. For the first time in his life, all of extraordinary possibility open and no Semitic prohibition, Jesus could freely speak. He could listen now at leisure to the lives of others, hear at length the inner voice of the soul in each individual met. A clear-minded, strong and free man abroad in the world and closer by now to a more mature possession of himself, he could speak from more of himself to the source of truth in everyone.

Still anchored at Joppa and helping to fit out their ship, Jesus met a young tanner, a Philistine, Gadiah. Day's work on the ship over, they went walking under the palms. Crunching pumpkin seeds by the warm sea at dusk, they talked. Like many other people, his new friend Gadiah, opened to him. Neither man caring for the stalling gambits of chat, they plunged right in to what interested them both, ethics and truth. Gadiah told him a story from the Bible. It always intrigued him, he said, the one about Jonah to whom God gave a message to take to Nineveh. The story was that Jonah refused, strayed off into a wanderer's life, went here, went there, fell off a ship's deck, was gulped down by a whale, lived in its belly, and there suffered. When Jonah was ready to take the message to Nineveh, the whale spewed him out on the shore.

By the thundering surf at Joppa the two chuckled with pleasure at the story.

Gadiah asked, "Do you think the whale really swallowed Jonah? What's your interpretation of it?"

"Aren't we all Jonahs?" parting his hands, Jesus smiled as they strolled beneath the palms, "It's a story of flight. Escaping life's service, we are swallowed by the whale of selfishness. So, there we sit," he made a hand sketch of the image, "in the belly of the dark. But if you ask for light with a whole heart, the whale deposits you on your own doorstep, on the shore of a fresh start."

The way the man's arms parted, it looked to Gadiah, like it was for the whole world. "But I've a question," he confessed, "It's the question of my life. Tell me, this is serious; how can God, if he is good, permit evil? Does God create it?"

Jesus and Gadiah talked. Evil, said Jesus, only existed because the revelation of the Infinite to the world was incomplete. Reality had been so arranged that humans could choose from it, truth or error. But no, Jesus stressed, God did *not* create evil. The small and unreal things of evil couldn't exist in God. "Evil is unreality, all it is, is error. And as such, evil has no universal standing. Evil doesn't even exist," he said, "not until a human chooses it. That's why on this plane, evil and good exist together, just as the tares may grow with the wheat until the harvest."

At Caesarea. They were mending the paddles of the ship. A Greek shipmate, hammering away next to Jesus, leaned over to him and said, "Listen, wise one, give me advice; there's a foreman of my crew, he keeps tormenting and pestering me. He's lewd, a red-neck, a slave driver, you know the type, the sort to laugh at cruelty. If the Gods care for me, O Hebrew teacher, why do they allow it?"

"Listen friend, have you ever thought, `What if the Gods put this man in my way for me to be a help to him'?"

"No." The Greek hadn't. He never thought of it.

"So maybe," this Jew was saying, "if you are more blessed with truth, then your job is to help him to it. This could be an adventure for you, to be the man's partner in his struggle. I'd bet if you had a word with him, the good in you would win him over."

That night the Greek had a try. He ambled across the deck to the overseer. The man was looking odd, bent over there by the ship's stern staring, ugly and morose, into the waves. The Greek repeated what that Jesus fellow had said. The Roman shot a look at the Greek. Both of them tired, they sat down in the sea wind on the deck. One man had some wine, none too good, but wine none-the-less, and poured some for the other as they discussed their odds and ends over a few mugs of it. The Roman let slip a few bits about his gory past, the Greek about the island from where he came, the Roman about a bull dog he once had, the Greek about a girl he wanted to marry, the Roman about the woman who left him, and, "Here, amigo! Hold out your cup; have more wine!" After some hours the two of them, by now sashaying about arm in arm, found Jesus still worrying at a winch on the deck. Over more wine and a few salt herrings this time, the three went on talking for hours in the nightlight as their ship ploughed on, over and into the dawn's coral colored waves.

Young Ganid was quite taken by Jesus. How come, he wondered, such a sophisticated Jew, a man of such presence and of implied power, spent his leisure with people, nobodies, from whom he had nothing to gain? So, one evening the lad asked, "Say, Yeshua, why are you so interested in strangers?"

His teacher, a frequent smiler, now had to laugh outright, "Ganid, under God there are no strangers! Everyone is kindred. Do you know," in a fraternal move he leaned to Ganid, "in the whole entire world what the most unimaginable pleasure is? It's getting to know another human being."

Next, they docked in Alexandria. In the library of the legendary city they saw the collection of nearly one million manuscripts from the world, from Greece to Japan. Leafing through the tomes, Ganid was surprised, but then not, that the world's religions all more or less recognized a universal God.

In Alexandria's blended cultural air, Jesus proposed they go to hear that Hellenist-Judaic master, the noble Philo speak. But their luck was out—Philo lay a-sick with chills in bed. In the lecture hall of Alexandria's museum, they listened to the proudly eloquent perorations of the world's most learned men.

"But, but, but," in the emptying auditorium, spluttered Ganid after a dissertation, "compared to you, my Yeshua teacher, these philosophizers are befogged! Please, let them hear you! Speak to them!"

Jesus clapped his young friend on the back, "Ganid, they are not so minded that I should." Yet, as he said this, Ganid noted, it wasn't with a skerrick of rancor.

Observing those worldly disquisitors, Ganid saw, they did indeed possess the finicky pride of a learning that refused the spiritual. These were the self-assured. They clung to their own values, wouldn't go beyond them, refused to imagine anything they didn't already know, or ever let their thought to be led, or ever conclude in God.

In Alexandria a city of much effect, Ganid who was always itchy to talk of reality's ultimates, wanted to know his tutor's views.

A generously attributing person, Jesus said, "As Plato himself might have put it, a cause cannot be less than its effects. Just so, Ganid, you cannot derive the refined lives of humans from a cause less than that life itself. You can't get spirit from mindless matter. Intelligence and complexity cannot be explained by anything less than complexity and intelligence. The very fact that humans experience a God transcending themselves is a sign that God lives in humans."

"Take self-consciousness. That humans progress, that people actually grow in spirit, how can there be an awareness of spirit without a universe of spirit as its foundation? Nor can a personality experience divinity without it being caused by divinity itself. The only proof of God on this earth is that the personality can experience him and can receive him into itself. Personality is the most unique thing about a person—not their status, nation, or group. Personality is the new communion, a mystery born of itself. Personality points to the Creator."

"Say more," begged Ganid, charmed.

"God," said Jesus, "universally and continuously expresses eternal realities. These shed cosmic light. Imperfect beings stand in the way of it and eclipse that light. Perfection is a being attuned to the universe. To be perfect is merely to be real. Not conforming your life to the universe's trends ends in your personal separation from it. And the real story of any life is the way you move towards the perfect love-grasp of its source, the Universal Father."

This was the substance of their talk.

Next, they anchored at Lasea in Crete. With Gonod busy at markets and business, Jesus and Ganid took to the high mountain trails of the Cretan wilderness. Climbing about, they tramped on for hours and saw the shiest of plants, spurge, sumac, rock-cress. They caught whiffs of the aromatic germander, found dwarf gorse among a crop of rocks. Quince trees punctuated a scene of bristling texture, pines, spikes of cypresses, black junipers and asphodels in the grass. In a clearing Ganid spied an exotic dog-rose. The conifers of mountain-fir bobbed about in the brisk breeze. Pine needles twirled on the wind, each needle a shivering jet of shine.

Tramping on, and pepped up by all this, they met a person on the track. He was a young boy, a Greek, just sitting there naked, right there, on a rock. His face down, his features were smudged. It was as if living alone had made him blur over. He looked as if he would rather be a rock, or even a spiky hedgehog, than face some unbearableness. He had the face of a person of no family, no community, no context. Too much aloneness had made him vague. Instead of sharpening his character, solitude had blunted it. There was an unreality about him, a thing intangible, even half-mad. One glance at that lost face, and Jesus saw what it was, the depression of one isolated from humans.

He strode right up. He wished the boy the joy of the day. When he didn't reply, Jesus, taking no note of the rebuff, asked him about a trail towards Phoenix in the mountains. Refusing the greeting, the young man met the request for help. He bent to the ground and drew on the soil, explaining each path and valley, bit by bit, careful. Bending to the dust-map, Jesus lightly said, "You know, friend, there *are* trails of happiness out of this."

A certain tone in the Jew's voice let the young Cretan recognize help in his path. "How?" he asked.

"Look at your assets!" Jesus said, "You've better than average strength. And your mind is your best resource. Use it to think its way out of sadness. Look, I know, you do have hurdles. And you have had a real thwarting. But it's past. Listen, the real things of the universe are on your side. Your mind is clear, it's capable. Use it to look at the spirit in you—that's your real potential for a great life. Choose a life of service. Just choose it. Serve others. It will free you from the helpless inferiority you felt. Have faith in that inner life of yourself. Do it for humans, for the sake of God. And you will see, as you act, you will be readjusted to the universe."

For a few moments, the three stood at that spot in the Cretan woods. They looked out and above on an Aegean sky of every shade of blue. From their ridge of purplish bronze rocks, there seemed no need for more words.

Fortune was this young man's name. After that meeting on the mountains with the Jewish traveller and his Indian friend, Fortune re-entered the world. He found he wanted to stay with it after all, to live in its body, be with its people, not to be separate.

And quite a while later, he was to become a leader of Crete's growing believers in a Hebrew healer from Palestine. One of the things Fortune found himself drawn to, was this teacher calling himself "Son of Man." It suggested the nature of what he taught. Fortune embraced with relish the "Life-Abundant" practices of a healer, whose teachings he liked so well, but whom, alas, Fortune never knew, or met.

Or, so he thought.

Another fascination for Ganid was how almost everyone was drawn to his tutor. Once walking the roads of Crete together, he slipped into step, "Can you tell me, my rabbi, why do you like everyone? How can I, too, make friends?"

"Be interested in people!" Yeshua flung back lightly from his stride, "See what you can do for them."

Times were, Ganid would take a long look at this man and see in him that ideal older brother he might have had. His was a manner of such inexpectant lightness, the buxom approach and ease of a man independent of others, and always himself. Also, and Ganid observed this without logically understanding it, Jesus had a healing in him, simply because of what he was. It was just there in him, a creative force. And though he performed no miracles, unhappy people, the ill, the strange, the wretched and alien, were drawn to him. All he would do is look at you, as tides of sheer love would come from his person and go straight to your heart. When he talked, he made you aware of the great surrounds in which you were set, and you became happy just from becoming aware of that. When troubled people heard him, they felt re-linked, put back on track, back in the world, returned to themselves. What a rehabilitator he was!

In Carthage they met a priest of the Mithraic religion. Both Jesus and the Mithraist being objective-minded men, they got on very well. After a meal shared in the priest's home they began on a subject of philosophic interest to them both—Time.

Said Jesus, the motion of time was revealed by a timeless sense orientating man. Events viewed from the outside seemed to be in a sequence. But as you deepen, your time-sense would branch. Reality expands. Linear time moves towards a sense of its circular simultaneity. "In the experiencing of time," he said a new thing no one had till then, "there are mansions of the cosmos in which humans are destined to achieve their identity. No, don't look like that!" he laughed at their baleful faces, "It means you don't have to make yourself perfect here, you don't have to do it, get yourself right once and for all. It is only on the attainment of full understanding that humans really make any sense. Your true place of operations is in the Absolute. Only with God do you find your true place in the Universe."

During their time together, Ganid saw Jesus give care to people. Everyone mattered to him. He was always wanting to say, especially to those who had lost heart, a few very good things about who in reality they are. "The most vital thing about you," Ganid heard him say, "is your future, not your past. Your Spirit Father is your absolute basis, your real coherence point; if you don't get it right here, never fear, in God your future is very good." He was also saying something many people couldn't even imagine in that place—that there was no soul-death; your soul went on and it did not go to waste. You were not an off-cast or a by-product of the material universe as the acid-styled philosophers liked to say. Jesus spoke of an infinity of lives to come, outlining our true universe environs, people's real future, and frame. He said, your soul did not snuff out, it didn't extinguish, not even into God. That your soul became sharper, more exactly itself in a tremendous project of expansion, performance, exertion, and none of it alone, but related and together with others.

At the very least, Ganid saw, Jesus made you put this question to yourself; "If what this man is saying about God is an illusion, what exactly is the proof for it? And why could the opposite not be the case?"

"Therefore," Ganid went on nutting it out, "if, on the logical plane there is no material proof for either of these stands, no proof for God, and none against, what is the basis for being on either side?"

Your own disposition seemed to be the answer.

Jesus, thought Ganid, he gave you a choice. A creative choice between ultimate goodness and ultimate meaninglessness. So, though prone to the sceptical, Ganid decided, "May as well go with the creative alternative. You could go somewhere with the pro-eternity choice, the good and the meaningful and the forever, and nowhere at all with the other."

From Crete they set out to sea once more. This time their ship was sailing through the straits, out to sea to many hours of ploughing the waves, then back to harbour and landing on Appian earth.

For nearly a week they were in Syracuse, where they met a Jew named Ezra. He too, was a man in big soul-trouble. His was the worst, a feeling of total absence gnawing a hole in his life. Ezra's words for it were, "I cannot find God."

Listening to him at length, Jesus felt for the man's emptiness. But Ezra's being a mature soul, he could say to the man, "Even your hurt itself is evidence that you have found God. Your pain means God has found you already. Your trouble is, you do not *know* God. But don't despair, for you shall. Just keep at it. Do you know those words of Jeremiah, 'You shall find me when you shall search for me with all your heart?'"

These scant words given in Syracuse by the sea, were enough to satisfy the lean soul of Ezra.

At Messina Jesus bought three melons and a bag of juicy apples from a boy. He gave the fruit-boy, but a child, the cheer of a blessing to last for life, "Just have courage, lad," Jesus touched his hand to the boy's hair, giving it a brotherly tug, "feed your body. Also the soul. Eat and pray. And Heaven's Father will go before you."

Once in Naples, Ganid had a surprise. His tutor always spoke full-heartedly with everyone. But here, he gave a coin to a beggar, and then just passed by. He always stopped to swap a few words with any man or woman in plight. But turning back, Ganid saw the beggar had no focus point in his eye. That center spot of self-cognition was absent, his mind not there.

And Naples was sublime—the epic blue span of the bay, its rocky ring of volcanoes, the expanse of sloping planes and sky. Soon they were mazing up through Italy toward Rome, the center of the civilized world. It was an easy, flat, and wonderful road where, fleet-footed, shaded, and sunned, upon the three travellers went. They walked along singing beside their pack-animals, smiling their greetings on hundreds of children, women and men, as they went on whistling along the Appian Way.

*Chapter VI*

# Rome

Rome was a world ready for Heaven.
 Contrary to the Hebrews' malignings, Rome was not a haunt of butchers or maniacs. Rome was a world ready for a change of heart. As the footsore three stood by the city's threshold their senses were seized by it. Rome was imposing—magnificent bastions and gates, broad avenues with ringing Latin names like Via Sacra, Ostian and Servillian, the Marine Theater, the river Tiber, the Lucullus Gardens, and the Circus near the Palatine. In well-appointed districts were colonnaded estates in landscapes of marble and cypresses, flanked by groves of poplars and chestnut. In Rome were the Gymnasia, much frequented by hedonists for risqué fun, but despised by the city's ethical patrician tone. Held in equal stentorian odium were the disreputable baths. As for the despicable Coliseum built for the imperial blood-sports, it was pooh-poohed by the well-bred and refined. Nobly crowning one of the seven hills was the undisputed civic glory of Rome, the Hill of the Palatine.
 Moving about Rome, Jesus was amazed. The tone of the city was an arms-open metropolitan commodiousness—not the hell-hole of brutes and swine that Palestine's Jews had said. Yes, power there was, but it was of politics and civil law. And yes, Rome was despotic, but spirit was separate, and no part of politics as in Palestine. There was no serious state-mandated religion—perhaps some stagy protocol of court-etiquette, an obeisance really, a silly scraping and bobbing to a yawning Caesar as "god," which, in Rome's more sober days embarrassed any sane man. But soul

was ungoverned. So it was free. Rome having no monomaniacal exclusivist beliefs, faith was personally and freely chosen and therefore morally interesting. In Rome's academies much of public discourse had been shaped by the Greek language which had given Rome's philosophers a fitting tongue in which to speak of superb things; truth and perfection, spirit over matter, justice, virtue, eternity. The mind-set of antiquity had long insisted that the divine rule the world, that some absolute good be the foundation of the cosmos. Greek thought first made contact with the Absolute by demanding, first, purity of soul, then integrity of mind. The Pythagoreans had long said there was an archetypal reality, law-based, predictable and unified, to be revealed by disciplined discourse. The whole tenor of this was the opposite of Semitic assertion with its yen for the uncaused and underived, ending in a penchant for the arbitrary, a slavering for miracle and marvel. The Greek method was by observation, its subject the Ideal, Eternal Ideas and Forms. Greek thought posited goodness, truth and beauty as the basis for knowledge, reason as the procedure, and tended to epiphany and luminosity, these being the intrinsic magnetic peaks that drew the classical mind. In Rome, it occurred to Jesus that with such a bent of soul and mind, the Empire's people might sooner receive his word than his own.

Gonod had several Indian translators here. So Jesus and Ganid were free. But first, a visit to the Palatine, and there, to the residence of the Emperor Tiberius.

Gonod bore greetings from India to the Emperor. Phlegmatic usually, at their entrance, Tiberius seemed to buck up. Deemed an unregenerate swine by Jews, Tiberius appeared to be weary, or merely gauche, even shy, and treated his three visitors very well. A diffident man of gray, clammy hands, he was surrounded by a brilliant court of military tacticians, schemers, bawds and wits all sharper than he, all bright Latinate conspirators. When his three visitors took their leave, already walking away, they heard Tiberius remark to his courtiers with wry wistfulness, "If I had that Jew fellow's bearing I might be a real Emperor, eh?"

In Rome Jesus had a project—how to present what he was to say. He plumped for the obvious. He sought out each religious leader, one by one, and asked if they could have a discussion. Each leader was delightedly surprised. An invitation to exchange ideas? Of course no one refused. Who would fob-off the chance to air, try out, maybe re-examine the truth by which you lived? That is, if it was a truth and not some crack-pot private mysticism that would shrivel if freed from the dungeons of privacy.

Jesus made friends with Rome's Mithraic, Cynic, and Stoic leaders, about thirty women and men. Pure minded, balanced, and very fervent people, the best of conversations happened with them. He found Rome's people vivacious, their hallmark, openness, having no settled opinion as to all future religious development. In their porous pan-spirituality he saw that by over-stressing the goodness of God, the Hebrews had excluded much of life; they had not valued beauty, character, science, or art. When Jesus spoke with Rome's priests and priestesses, it was never with more than three. Hardly anyone in Rome was hiding themselves in that dreary, strangulating game of national and religious identity. And each person was charmed by the "Jewish Tutor's" style. He never attacked flaw, he didn't keep hacking away at error, had no interest in proving you wrong but went with the gathering force of truth in a person's belief and built from there. On the flow of the positive in a person's mind, error was crowded out.

Angon was the first man he met, a leader of the Stoics. They talked of science and religion all night. Mardus was the next. A leader of the Cynics, and of elevated nature, Mardus wanted to talk of evil and good, a subject of concern to him.

Now, in a culture over-ripe, the words "good" and "evil" may be tedious. In Rome too, sophisticated people were saying things like: "It's all relative," and, "How can you know?" and, "Who cares?" The going philosophy was "Your life is your fate," which, in a couple of thousand years would recycle as, "Your genes/your DNA/your environment are your fate." Rome's leisured classes were also given to saying, "Life has no point" and "Life's not about anything," or "Life is just the things you touch." People there also liked to live in the surging of instincts and blood, which a future time would call "your hormones," or, "your bio-chemistry" or, fatalistically, "your karma." They disdained the inquiry after causes, hating words like "truth" as well, preferring to slide off into the aesthetic, saying things like, "Only beauty counts," or "the random smile of a stranger." They were saying then too, that belief in the unseen was a disorder of the mind, a form of grovelling for what you already had, a suicide of the intellect. That devotion to a limitless God was silly because the world provided no proof for it. Loving your own present was alone practical, so they valued only their own sensations, scorning "good" and "bad" as boring and uncivil.

But Mardus, a more seriously practical person, wanted to thoroughly hear of them.

# Rome

Of good and evil, in the company of Mardus, Jesus said, "These words only signify what a human is able to understand of the universe. As humans grow, the more of goodness is experienced. In fact, a person's development is proportionate to their ability to see good."

"So," asked Mardus eager to conclude on a point, "what *is* the good?"

"Good," said Jesus, "is whatever helps you realize your moral self. It is your own spirit that is always orientating you to the reality of the universe." And goodness, he said, though a personal experience, it *was* linked to truth.

Of truth, he said, it was the divinely real. But these were just words, the verbal gesture at essence, and words couldn't define truth, only the living of it did that. Yet the truth revealed was the spirit's highest delight. It was the mind focusing on reality. But any part of focused reality was only an abstraction, not the whole of it, and alas, truth tends to be dogmatized by fear and laziness. There was no truth without faith, Mardus was to remember him saying, "Faith is the inspiration of the spiritualized creative imagination."

In Rome Jesus met Nabon, a Greek Jew. This man asked him what everyone was always asking, "What is the purpose of human life?"

In essence, Jesus said why human life began, and why it goes on after death is because life has a function in the universe. The purpose of humans is to achieve God, and a soul cannot stop growing before reaching the destiny for which it was made. Once the goal is reached it cannot end because by then the soul is like God, eternal. The presence of God in the human mind is the pledge of life's continuation.

He said every soul seeking God goes on forever because, by that act, you become *real* to the universe. Personality goes on developing forever; its increasing freedoms matched by self-restraint. Complete spiritual self-control leads to complete universe liberty.

Jesus lived six months in Rome. How he spent his time and the sort of things he did for the people he met was how he would be for the rest of his life. His message in Rome was what it would always be— "God loves you; he loves each human being; he is the Father of your spirit; the spirit-home of everyone."

As for the people he met, who were, after all, the point of this whole expedition—they found Jesus an affectionate man. He had great esteem for people. He always treated them as if he *knew* they were good, and he knew the absolute worth of each person to Heaven. And this cheered people up.

## His Real Life

This was his focus, his most enthusiastic point. It worked like a tonic; it got people up, got them going above themselves. Many of Rome's pagans were already highly ethical women and men. But on meeting Jesus they felt what most people there never did—they felt their soul opening, and praise, the one thing missing, the "Alleluia" dimension, entered into their existence. Yet, he was no savant, no seer, no celebrity. He overwhelmed no one. No one who heard him was ever thunderstruck. Talking to him, people found themselves not soothed or coddled, but spurred to make contact with their own real will. He led people to their own decisions by showing you *could* choose your fate. He brought people to a clarification of who they were, to their essence, to their own experience of it.

Neither did he evade or side-step the real questions people always asked: Does life have a meaning? Shall we live after this? What is best? Is it the same for everyone? Are we remembered? Cared for? Loved? And people did ask these things of him; they asked it of one another, and all the time. Those who came to him were indeed, often the weak, the needy and distressed, those left behind by the speed of life. He listened to these flattened ones, and they were glad, just to have someone who heard them with accuracy and compassion, without any corrupt taking of sides.

His first way of help was practical suggestions. Next, the causal, the immediate, the small and useful steps. If you were at the end of your tether he reminded you, no, you're not useless, or irrelevant, or an idiot, but loved. You mattered, and very dearly, to your soul-parent, the Creator God. That, he reminded you, was the framework in which you lived. In God, he said, was the level that humans really made sense. And this, he told them, is the universe's actual, logical, factual and functioning structure.

In Rome he spoke to all sorts; to a soldier, a statesman, a physician, an orator, giving the advice for which each one had asked: How to deal with wealth? To whom give it? What was fair? What was not? And was Man more than a body? And was the soul real, the realest part? And how to have courage; how to show mercy; love beauty, and how to reach out to God? His was a naive and innocent way, but one of great power, especially for the untaught and ignorant who more often had the broken simplicity of heart to just put out their hands without being scared to be a fool for a gift from God.

Atheists fascinated Ganid. Apart from the poor, the bunglers and the inept (for whom Jesus may have more tenderly cared because of the longing of their hearts,) Rome also had those people asleep in whom no question about ultimates had ever woken. These were the placid, the leave-well-alone types who couldn't bear to be wrong or tricked. They were the nature worshippers who saw their god as romantic, poetic, even mystical but by no means to be any more than a pet aspect of themselves. And there were the aesthetes who lived for beauty alone, believing they were being mentally tidy and modest to settle for a life of mere perception. Despite the dignity of its pagan order, Rome had no vision, no depth of life, no living heart. Like the aimless wit of its weary farceurs, even the highest of Roman virtues left out the vital dimension, spirit. Some of that world tried substituting soul with sex, believing sex to be "honest," a part of existence. Alas however, as found even by its aficionados, sensuality by itself went nowhere, only back into yourself dying there of privacy and brevity—a dead-end. Even that world was finding sex had no proposition, no development about it, no pole-vault into the infinite. But such, grimly declared Rome's philosophers, was the nature of the world. And though desiring the enlargement of consciousness, they resisted its endeavor. They were irked by suffering and despised both humility and hope. They preferred the heroic stiff-lipped putting-up with existential emptiness. They insisted on the mentally elegant posture of resistance, preferring the dignity of composure to the ungainliness of faith. The posture of belief left you discomposed, and the adoration of the Invisible was abject, lacking the *sangfroid* of Cool. Resignation was somehow dignified, while the ardor of faith made you look a fool.

Therefore, Ganid was not really surprised when his tutor said, "You can't give to those who are not hungry." Of Rome's unbelievers Jesus said, "No point in engaging those who don't ask. Their minds are already satisfied."

Concerning self-satisfaction, Jesus was also thinking of the Hebrews. Neither romantics nor sensualists at all, Jews had the Law, and knew thereby the universal lot. And knowing they knew, they did not like hearing of anything new. Of Rome's rag-bag of gentiles, who, having nothing, were quick to hear and ask, Jesus remarked in an incidental tone as they passed through the crowds, "The way to live, Ganid, is so that the Father can live through our lives."

Later, on excursion to the North, the three were in the mountains of Switzerland. In a relaxed mood, Gonod asked, "What of Buddha, dear Master, your opinion of him, I'd like to know it."

"He was a great man," Jesus reflected against the noble jags and horns of the Swiss mountain land, "but he was an orphan prophet. He had a good

## His Real Life

life-philosophy. But no God. Yet Buddha did know God in his spirit. The super-conscious in Buddha was Godward, but not his mind. Jews know God with the mind, but not well in spirit. Buddha lacked a vision of God, and so did not give a teaching with the spirit drive of a world-religion to exalt the generations."

"Let's you and I make a religion!" Ganid, a boy forever, cried, "A religion good enough for India and big enough for Rome!"

Jesus roared laughing. He ruffled his young friend's hair. A new religion! What you don't realize, Ganid, is that what you most want to do in spirit, you are doing already. And so it is with any human being—that which the spiritual imagination most wants to do and be, becomes active to the degree that human is dedicated to the doing of the Father's will.

*Chapter VII*

# The Return from Rome

He left Rome as he had come to it, no fuss, no ceremony. Enough that he had come to know and love a lot of people there. An entire year passed before his Roman friends gave up hope of seeing him again. But as time went by, an odd serendipity, but they found themselves gravitating towards each other. Chance meetings and street corner chats, and his friends found they were visiting each other. As friendships grew, the talks around family hearths, they found Jesus had been their meeting-point. Wasn't it amazing! He had been their convener really; he had rallied them, he rounded you up, called you in, a shepherd. They found themselves wondering about his future. He was a man to have crowds listen to him for the big or small, but always stirring things he said. Meeting at one another's houses, his friends recalled their times with him. "What a man!" they were agreed, "What deep virtue and innocence! He was so real, the realest person." He had created an impact of such reality on them, and they yearned for him in memory with a poetic sort of nostalgia.

But he, by now long on route with his two Indian friends, had been light-stepping along Italy on the Appian.

Once during their hike, Ganid, preferring the Hebrew name of his teacher, asked, "Yeshua, what's your opinion of the caste system of India?"

"You can't help the differences in ability of skill and mind. But to the universe, Ganid, there are only two classes: those who know God, and those who do not."

Near Tarentum they walked into a brawl. A smallish boy was being bashed by a big thug. Without a thought, Jesus jumped in. He flung himself on the bully, held him fast, so the boy tore free. Then Jesus let the basher go too. Grabbing the lout, Ganid started dispensing the resonant wallops of righteousness. But Jesus stopped Ganid. And the thug fled.

"I don't get it!" Ganid gasped, "You saved the boy! But doesn't justice say the bully should be punished?"

"It's true you don't get it!" After the tussle, Jesus was brushing himself into place, laughing with relief, "Use mercy as an individual, Ganid! But leave justice to the group. Mercy is lavish, from the heart. Justice is precise. But you know, in an organized universe sentence is only passed by those who know all the facts."

This was just one of those times that Ganid noticed yet again; when speaking of this earth, Jesus included a whole network of world, of a huge and wide-flung universe. His presumption of a massively extended physical organization expanded the vast moral inclusion of persons involved. At this point, Jesus told Ganid there was a perfect technique of universal reflectivity on the constellations of worlds on high, an exact cosmic mechanism for knowing the exact motives of minds.

Ganid, a boy to naturally admire force and heft, was intrigued by his teacher's attitude to power. Despite he had the steely body of a laborer, after all, Jesus was a strapping carpenter and smith, a muscly fisherman, he took no part in physical fights.

"Not even in self-defense?" queried Ganid from under the tall pines of the Appian where they went. "What if you were attacked? What's if it's life or death?"

On this occasion his tutor hesitated. "Well," he looked awkward, as if too hard to visualize. But not given to dismissing other's questions, he said, "Before doing everything to save my life, I would have to be convinced my attacker was not fully human."

"What's a 'not fully human'?"

"One who cannot know God."

"But if he could? Would you just let him kill you?"

"Ganid," his friend sighed at the hypotheticality of it, "I have in me a life-task. If the work is from God, I cannot believe real harm can come to it. If the work is his, the Father will take care of it. And our enemies will not be able to harm it. And what shall we fear from our friends? There is an all-powerful truth I really believe," he said with rare intensity, "the universe is friendly to us, despite it sometimes looks otherwise."

"I suppose," smiled Ganid, "someone or something will always defend you."

"Why do you think that?"

"Because you're that nice."

"The test," Jesus flung an arm about the young man's shoulders as they marched on their way, "has yet to come."

At the port of Tarentum, a repulsive sight—a man cuffing his wife about the ears. And she, true to the era's norms of pathos and long-sufferance for women, took it weeping, wailing, a victim. Jesus wanted to rush straight to her, spur her to act, but the principle of the feminine still half-asleep in history, he had first to go to the man, then still the active influence. Jesus put a hand on him. Lurched out of momentum, the man stopped thrashing his wife. He thought, "This stranger has to be a priest, to butt in like that!" And next, he found himself being taken by the elbow.

"What's the matter, friend? Your wife, what has she done?"

"Er, nothing really," croaked he, "She's a good woman. But hell! She gets on my nerves! Picking at me in public. I'm glad you stopped me, but …"

Laying an arm about the man's shoulder in companionable Levantine style, Jesus went walking with him. They strolled on the strand, about the port, cooling down. As they spoke, they touched on the subject of love, that how a man loves his wife was a mark of his spirit. That in creating children with immortal souls, a human pair become partners with God. "Sharing life on equal terms with your wife is a God-like act," Jesus said, "You know, just as God loves the Universe-Mother of their spirit children," he shook the man's shoulder and said it to his eyes, "so ought a man to love his wife."

The man was touched. In his own way, he thought much the same, himself. While back along the pier, his wife in her lilac veil was waving to him. And he to her.

Alas, too soon, the three travellers re-boarded their vessel, bound for Corinth.

On the quay of Tarentum stood his two new friends, re-paired in an embrace, waving and waving in the departing ship's wake.

Corinth. The third most cosmopolitan city of that world, people of every ilk and hue flocked to it. Like other liberal pagan centers, Corinth also saw sensuality's other face—sex severed from heart and soul degenerated into trashy business cynicism, the whipped egos and squalor of prostitution.

Also in Corinth stood an architectural feat, a twenty thousand feet high citadel above the sea. Ganid never tired watching the crowds milling under it, like watching the live planetary mosaic. Peering down at the shoals of harlots, the young Indian man wondered; his Hebrew tutor, Yeshua, not over-talkative but ready to speak when asked, why didn't he say anything about sex, not even a joke?

Ambling one night in the moonlight by the citadel, they passed two whores. Ganid, playing the prude, flung a wild, rude gesture at them.

"Listen," Jesus grabbed his arm. "Don't. Don't look down on them! Whatever they do, they are still the Father's children."

It stopped Ganid short. His tutor was saying, was he not, you weren't your acts. That, however sordid, no life was void of grace. Ganid tried to imagine the "grace" possible to a vendor of sex; could even evil provide a proof of the love of God? Did degradation reveal the distance between the human and the divine? Might even sin activate its opposite, or at least wedge out a gap into which God could come? Really, might even awfulness reveal love? A prostitute, Ganid went on thinking it out, she would certainly know the buyers of sex, men away from the humbug of social respectability. A whore would see males at their most base, tyrannical and lustful selves, see grown men turn into braying asses for sex, from which she might see the truth of herself, who she really was. Though intrigued by sex, Ganid could also imagine, that the life of a prostitute might not hide the truth, but reveal it. There could even be a miracle, even from business-sex; revolted and bored by it, a person might turn to that far greater mobilization, the passion of the soul for God.

"Listen Ganid," Jesus interrupted his musings, "how can we know, let alone judge, what led these women to this? There are people who choose low things; but look at them, isn't it clear? These women accepted this way to earn a living in an hour of hopelessness."

Ganid considered it. "I am sorry," he said. "In my spirit I apologize to them, I hope they forgive me."

"I think they do. As I think the Father in Heaven forgives them."

They approached the women. Speaking pleasantly a while together, Jesus asked, how would they like to meet some people at the home of Justus, a widely known merchant of Corinth? He lived quite close, just here by the synagogue. Winded by the Hebrew's courtesy, the prostitutes darted

## The Return from Rome

baffled looks at each other. In his presence, the older one no longer felt she had to put on the humble-furtive act of poor women. Nor did the other have to feign respect for masterful men. With these two, they could be, not obsequious, but themselves. Both women nodded a come-what-may "Yes, thank you" to the invitation.

Martha, the wife of Justus, came to the door. Her husband not at home, she was surprised by the lateness of the hour, what with Jesus dropping in with prostitutes . . . but no moralizing conventionalist, she laid a table of homely food for them. During the meal, all going so well, Jesus suddenly stood up. "We shall now leave you together, you three women—you, the beloveds," he smiled happy and passionate, "beloveds of the Most High. Ganid and I," he thumped his friend's back, "we pray you make good life-plans for the future."

Shortly afterwards, the older woman died. But by then she had been in service a while to the household of Justus and Martha. She died a woman made ready, a person shifted and changing, and in good hope. The younger one became a worker in Justus's business. She was an accountant, kept the books straight and right, and continued honing her mathematical skills. Later, she was to be one of the first members, and then a leader, of the early Church in Corinth.

Ganid couldn't get over it! How *did* Jesus make such contact? And with just anyone! He touched people, at first a little, and then later, their lives changed from the depth. He made you see that what you did mattered. So did how you felt. He showed how your acts were linked to your ideas, and that your thought was free, that what you chose of beauty and belief came from your soul and also actually shaped it.

From all their journeys together Ganid was to recall, when speaking to a person, Jesus used the language of that person's life. To a miller his tutor had spoken of the grains of truth, their grinding to make what was hard, to be like milk for the spiritually young.

To a Roman centurion, he heard Jesus say, serving God and Caesar did not conflict, not if Caesar didn't take the things of God. "Faithfulness to God could also mean devotion to a good Emperor."

Never bidding women to be the deferential caretakers of men, he said to a serving woman at a Greek inn, "Drudgery is an art if you offer it to the God who you know lives in each of your guests."

To a Chinese merchant he was heard saying, "The direction of your soul is Heavenward, to your true spirit-ancestor. So follow the spirit direction in yourself. But for now, farewell until we meet in the worlds of light, the delightful worlds God has prepared for pilgrims on your way to Paradise."

To a traveller from the North that was Britain, he said, "You seek truth. But it's already with you; you have the Father's spirit within. Listen, friend, have you ever tried to talk with your own soul's spirit? I know it is hard, and you may not see the results. But your mind's every attempt is imprinted in your soul which shall one day become a conscious experience."

On all their journeys Ganid saw, Jesus liked everyone. He came to people's problems, met them where they were. He didn't just listen, or ever re-cast the question you had, but put to you an alternative, showed you the real world, gave the best proposition of your life, "You are God's," he would say, "Divinity is your destiny." Then gave the steps of how to bring your acts in line with your intention, how to do it right.

Ganid could see, doing what Jesus recommended would call you to your will, it would ask for some pushing of mind and flexing of hearts. The call for you to take your real place did ask for effort. And there would always be those who preferred to languish in delay, thrash around in the emotional shallows of their easier selves. You could see why. The animal level was timid, it didn't ask for much. A life of splashing around in your instincts avoided the exercising of yourself. But it was an inert, a sleepy life that lay down in a snore before the exertion of a soul-migration to the higher grounds re-located for human identity by Jesus.

From Corinth they were sailing to Athens, the crown of the Aegean. Lunging out from the shore, their ship hemmed and darted in the waves. They skirted humps of fawn land in a sometimes wine colored sea. Bread-blond islands bobbed in the watery perspectives, a regatta of loaves on the sea. Until one blue morning it approached in white light—Athens. What a burst of beauty!

From their disembodied days on water, Athens rushed at them; striding vistas, spanning spaces, oval plazas, columns, temples, arches, pillars, octagons. Athens was a full frontal epic of a God-scene, huge sky, mountains, sun-lit marble, the scintilla of splendor. Above the city, that floatation of grace, the Acropolis hovered on top. If Greece had one visual symbol for its psychic focus, it was the Parthenon. Elate up there, Jesus strode about in the large spaces, the pale verticals and fluid lines of the temple thrilling him.

## The Return from Rome

Up there on the city's great rock he could see from the Greeks' sense of proportion that their minds were prone to both the causal and the numinous. Their sights already set to the sublime, a Son-from-God would seem not heretical, but very likely to them. A messenger of Son-Spirit status would be logical for Greeks as an expression of the Divine. With their pantheon of divinities, the Greeks would easily grasp his dual nature; they could instantly fit the revelation of God-in-Man with the inspiration of their ancient traditions and myths.

The priests of Palestine distrusted human nature so much that God's manifesting as Man would be a pagan vileness to them. But to the Greeks who saw gods in humans all over the place, God-in-Man would make pristine and blessed sense, the transformation of the one into another being quite regular in their myths. Their minds already given to epiphany, Greeks would have no trouble with the concept of "Christ," and could put epiphany into terms that would make it be known to the world. It would be Greeks to first organize a Scripture and church to establish a symbolic system that would survive the millennium, and even perhaps the one after that. It was the Hellenes who had perfected mathematics and logic, whose icons and symbols were of the most saintly idiom to first see the God-Man manifestation as both likely and possible. Because Greeks would stress the God-Man's ascendance over suffering, they would have his resurrection speak of creature existence and its endlessness. To the Greeks the Christ would be *Christos Anesti*! —Christ Risen. And this would be their achievement for the spread of faith on earth.

Up there, on the acropolis, Jesus foresaw the chances of this evolution with calm. Turning now from that elevated altitude, he walked on down into the town. Hopping over grass clumps and skirting ridges he turned once. Looking out over the land, he saw, a roar of tragic light. Athenian light spoke of universal yearning. It was the same light as over Rome, poised in preparation for the sublime. As Jesus descended through terraces of marble to a ground of asphodel and cypress he entered oriental din and chaos. Athens down here was slums and songs, donkey smells, a pother of merchants, touts and cats, basil, beggars, hawkers, scholars, disputants, everybody milling about. He felt the exaltation of the human here, the Greek zest for the world ambient. Boys did their shenanigans in the street. Young girls squealed and ballyhooed, allowed to be their madcap selves. Women at work joked and sang, their strong lovely hair not always covered, slapping washing on a fence running with the velvet trumpets of morning glory on it. At evening from the trellised courtyard of their tavern lodgings he looked out at Mount Hymetus. As dusk encompassed the city in tides of bronze and evening blues, he fell to wondering if such favoring beauty might have fitted Greeks to be such prompt receivers of truth?

Gonod having less of trade here, the three of them were visiting the sites of pilgrimage and art. If the morale of a culture can be judged by its art, then the culture of Greece was very high. Pagan devotional shrines were decorated by the votive statues, often of the sun god Apollo, and of Aphrodite, the goddess of love. On looking at them, it was obvious; the public art of Greece was not a psalm to any priapic frenzy or rabid sex. The sculptures of the gods brought to the beholder a view of the most touching humanity linked with empyrean stateliness. That pure look in the eyes of statues, the remote, abstract brow of heroes, the chill pure gaze of the gods, none of it was a paean to excess, but an art, contemplative and pointing beyond the senses. This was the quality of the statues, especially of Athena, the city's gray-eyed patron, the realms of pure good in her eye, solitary, always virgin, that is, undivided, an epitome of justice.

This idealism of the Hellenes, where had it come from? Their surrounds of nature? Their reverence for it? Could it be they looked out on their glorious seas and skies and felt that a beauty as extreme as this was a shadow of the greater reality behind it? This was the transcendent streak in the Greek psyche, fitting it with beauty to transmit a gospel of the human in the divine.

At their inn one evening the three were joined by a philosopher, long-winded and prolix. After the pundit had wound down his peroration—in three hours he didn't stop for a breath! —having listened courteously to his every word, Jesus spoke briefly of their theme; force, gravity, light. "But" he added in a relishing tone, "scientists will never be able to say what these universe phenomena are!"

For, he said, when the statistical egoism of science and the assertiveness of religion become tolerant, there will be a unified grasp of the cosmos. Yet even now, if one could see its actual workings, there *is* unity in it. The real cosmos, he said, was friendly to every child of God. The problem is, how can humans achieve a universe-knowing state of mind, one that corresponds to reality and be logical at the same time? "I think," he made one of those creative leaps that, though unprovable, work nonetheless, "only by conceiving the cause of both fact and value to be in the Paradise Father. I know this is an assertion, only to be taken on faith, but then, the first premise of any knowledge has also to be taken on trust. Faith alone unifies thought. It gives a purposeful unity to phenomena. Faith is the only faculty to reveal the goal of personality, God."

The pundit looked at Jesus. His pagan world was not immoral. It had the ethics of valor, candor, fidelity, respect, and public mindedness. But pagan thought had no convergence, no concluding point. To pagan humanity no point of infinite constructiveness had been proposed. The god-myths of Greece, though often sublime, did not lead the mind to the purpose it carved. The gods were many, but multiplicity did not gather psyche to a point. Nor did mythic polytheism provide the personal unity of a principled creation. The anarchic energy of paganism led to color, imagination, superstition, mood, emotion, flight—yes, very exciting, but all loose ends. The classical myths began the curve towards truth but did not bite through to reality, did not make the circle.

So, when this Greek scholar heard out the God-pointing reasoning of the young rabbi from Palestine, he mumbled, however grudgingly, "At last a Jew who talks of something other than racial superiority!"

In Ephesus. Drawn to its fluted and slender loveliness, the travellers visited the slim columned temple of Artemis. Later, at the school of Tyrannus, they were in a study room with another philosopher who heard Jesus mention "Soul." From perusing antique parchments, this sage turned to the Hebrew and said, "When you say 'soul,'" he challenged, "what do you mean?"

So, stimulated, the four sat down and spoke of it.

Soul, said Jesus, is the power in a person to see truth. Soul can think about itself. Soul knows spirit realities outside itself. And though self-consciousness alone wasn't soul, a moral self-consciousness was the soul's foundation.

"But there is such an entity as Spirit." Jesus made a gesture of distinction, "and it is *not* the same as soul. The spirit in a human is God's gift. Spirit comes *to* Man. It arrives at the first moral act of mind. The moment God's spirit comes to a human is the actual birth of the soul."

"A soul," said he, "could be lost or saved; salvation being nothing other than your own moral self-consciousness. Nor could you materially locate the soul. It wasn't open to any kind of spiritual proving either. Nonetheless," he said it smiling, "despite no science can prove the existence of soul, every human knows of the existence of his and her soul as a real personal experience."

After Ephesus was the long water voyage to Rhodes. For long stretches they enjoyed staring from the deck into the scattering foam, hours of water surfaces unravelling and knitting like lace. It seemed days later that they moored into port under Rhodian skies. The hues of Rhodes were roses in the morning, a wise jade green at night. One evening, Jesus walked alone on the shore line by himself. He saw two women meeting on the sea front under the promenade of acacias. The women embraced. Their hands fluttered over each other's faces, reminding him of his mother, her meeting with Elizabeth those years ago in the Nazareth yard, a tense significance in their expression as they listened to each other. His eyes lowered in reverie against the half lights of dusk. In a half whisper, he found himself uttering, "...John..."

After Rhodes their ship put in at Cyprus. Here was the lion-colored Homeric land. Cypriots were lit by charm; they were more oriental, less mercurial than mainland Greeks. Unemphatic sleepy folk just living inside their lives, they had an art of alluding power next to which the Hebraic literalism of his own people seemed arrogant. The sculptures of Cyprus seemed to say, "Behold here on earth the mystery of the Heavens, the praise of God by all beings and things," whereas Jews, who didn't understand the invocation of art, had squashed truth into the rigidity of precept, law, word and creed.

But then, you had to ask; what exactly did the Greek exaltation of beauty do for the person who suffered? What did beauty do for one in terminal pain? What of the one who had no beautiful body and was wrecked in it and could see no beautiful blue *thalassa* of a sea? The wisdom of beauty only warmed the already fortunate. It did nothing for the one in anguish, nothing for slaves; it didn't solve agony. From the Hellenic lands had come the existential view, "Eros and Thanatos run head to head in life." That being reconciled to the finitude of our mortality was truthful and brave. But did the holders of this view not see? It served only the powerful. That the logic of this proud message to the hopeless was only termination and end. No, beauty alone didn't speak to the craving for a God who heard you. And where in the Greeks' wisdom and beauty was the love of God for the individual?

Antioch. Speed and charge, spice and vice, such was Antioch, capital of the Roman province of Syria. A many-tongued city of half a million, there was a lot of trade for Gonod here. So Ganid and Jesus travelled about everywhere. The one spot to which Jesus would not go was to the notorious

## The Return from Rome

Grove of Daphne. Though Ganid and his father went to nose about there, prostitution in the name of religion was a repulsive mixture to their Hebrew friend, if not exactly all that shocking for world-wise Indians like themselves.

In Antioch Jesus seemed muted. When they asked him why, he only said, "We are close to Palestine. Sometime, I am to go back there." They realized then, though travel had been a pilgrimage for him to the physical world's everything, his homeland of Palestine had stayed within him. Both Indians were surprised not to have considered this in him, devotion, even homesickness, for the land of his origin.

Employed in Gonod's business in Antioch was a morose man. Disgruntled by his job, he was inept at it. A bungler, a ditherer and usually late, he lost keys, moneys, misplaced tools, consignments, he was a mucker really, and on the verge of being sacked. Ganid, who had by then gotten more of zeal than wisdom, sped to enlighten the man. At the assured top of his voice, youthful Ganid boomed out to this man his newly ringing ideals, not one, of course, having the least effect. That his trumpetings only succeeded in flattening the man left Ganid to wonder; was it the case perhaps, that there were simply no solutions to certain chosen soul-postures?

From Antioch they wound by camel-caravan down to the coastal Sidon. From here the desert unrolled. They reached sandy Ur, the archaic birth site of Abraham. From Ur to the ruins of Susa, Jesus set out on many trips, stimulated in that ancient land, probing history, ranging, exploring.

And then one day, the unimaginable came. Long having lived in travel's ravishing world together, the three wayfarers had to face it, the day of separation. The Indians had begged Yeshua to come to India with them. But, he said, having begun on Palestine's soil, he felt his life was to be about there.

So, by the port of Charax they stood about helplessly. Having to say a never-faced farewell, Gonod grasped his Hebrew tutor by the arms, "Thank you for everything. Especially for making us better human beings, and," he embraced the man, "for helping us to know God."

Suppressing tears in his eyes, his son, Ganid said, "I shall always remember you, my teacher, Yeshua. Heaven's Father must be like you. Or, from what you told us of God, you must be like him."

In the custom of the Orient, Jesus blessed his departing friends. A small boat carried them to their large ocean ship bound for the far East.

75

## His Real Life

From the shore he watched his friend's board. The large vessel heaved on and out to sea and left. While he stood on the shore, waving, waving.

So the young man and his father returned to India. As the years passed Ganid became there a man of business and influence. Sometimes, in company, he found himself absent-mindedly quoting, and then, with no program, spreading the insights he had learnt from Yeshua. At the time of parting in Charax, Ganid supposed that the searing inside him—it hurt so much he had no word for it—was just the pang of farewell. He did not know then that the wrench was a tear to last in him for the duration of a life. He didn't know that his missing of Yeshua would stay in him like a scar. And though the events of Ganid's life, his fortunate marriage and boisterous children might blanch the scar, he didn't count on the ache of it remaining in him. He never discussed it with a soul, and it never healed; that is, Ganid was never reconciled to it. And though at times it made him edgy, like a niggling, secret handicap, Ganid tried to never notice it. Certainly he never acted on it. Or not in public.

Still later, his achievements lauded, his marriage even happier and his children happy and numerous by then, at one of his opulent family celebrations Ganid heard some incidental talk about a teacher in a by then far-away and long-ago Palestine. People at his party were saying that this teacher had been called, "Son of Man," and in that savagely dogmatic world his teachings ended his life on a cross. Chancing to be a little step back from his circle of friends, Ganid fell to wondering, if only briefly, "What had that poor wretch of a teacher *done*?"

His friends were saying, "The Powers of Palestine accused the man of being a charlatan."

"Well, why . . ." with a shrug Ganid entered the conversation, albeit perplexed, "why would a mere phoney have upset the authorities so much? What on earth could that 'Son of Man' chap have said?"

"They charged him with being a 'perverter of Jewish truth.'"

Ganid pulled a face at "Jewish Truth," as ridiculous to him as "Jewish clouds," or a "Jewish blade of grass." "No, really!" he found himself beginning to insist, "What had the fellow done to deserve the extreme Roman method of execution?"

None of the Indians at his party possessing a mind to even imagine an answer to that, fell to prattling about the fellow's interesting, in fact, quite truly moving ideas.

*The Return from Rome*

Strangely. Ganid could never link the Palestine Jew on the cross with his Yeshua teacher and friend, now but a ghostly scar in himself.

Though before plopping another Turkish delight into his mouth, he recalled with a passing pang of surprise, their teachings sounded, well, really quite similar.

*Chapter VIII*

# Ready

When Jesus returned from Mesopotamia to Galilee it was December. He walked all the way back, the road a passion of his. The act of going, faring forth, all of movement, this was his heart's environment. In his thirties by now, journey had sharpened his senses, clearing his track. Travel had shown more of what was intended, that he live with the people and stay in unity with them. Though still free in the effacing pleasures of wandering, he was beginning to accept, his life-work would have to have a public phase. Into his drift through the bliss of anonymity came the realisation; he was to get ready.

So, he was going back.

From Antioch he tramped down the coast and stopped one morning to look upon Caesarea's bronze sea. The sea he saw as an illustration of his purpose, the waves unscrolling a testimony of their Source. On this land where every sparrow was a parable, the lilies a lesson, each river a pledge, even the brambles and thorns were so made as to be an analogue for the habits of God. From the shore he went down south to the villages, back to Joppa, then inland to Jamnia, Ashkelon and Gaza, and on to the desert lands of Beersheba. On his way back, he thought of his cousin, that pure and fiery man. In his prayers for John appeared ancient images of axe and fire, of annihilation and wrath. Even as youths they had both known, if John's message was to be about judgment, then his own would be about salvation, about being salved. If John's word was to be "Turn!" and "Repent!,"

*Ready*

his own would be about truth and its happiness. Not that these two movements were opposed in the soul.

Now he walked on further, out, alone on Palestine's sands and into the desert's lunar landscape. He passed Moab's metal-purple mountains beside the static glitter of the Dead Sea. Here he went, allured by the drizzling white haze of it. Through the vapor by the shore he saw groups of people talking by fires in the night. Knots of squalling kids ran about in the dark. When they saw him, they waved arms, they beckoned. So he went over and sat with them, everybody telling stories, eating, laughing.

He was not a man to talk much by now. But when he opened his mouth, people lifted their heads. He spoke, and they listened. Life came from what he said. When people heard him, they felt strife and ambition go quiet in them. They looked at him, and felt ferocity quench. He talked, and people saw God, right here with them under the moon's sheen. As they sat in the dark talking together, from somewhere a smell of unseen oleanders, and at midnight, a solitary cock's cry of "Eeee-Rieeeee!"

He could have gone on and on, and into what he would have so much liked, the walking-around life of a barefoot man who, having the invisible as his foundation, needed nothing else. But for all his land-walkings and distance covering he was going back, leaving the wide physical lands. It being hot now, he was walking at nights. From the hills the villages looked lit up, like necklaces on the dark's black neck. The cities he passed were jewels suspended in their own brilliance. And when after the leagues of flatness the land started rolling, hilly and greener near Nain he knew he was closer to Galilee. As he came back, he felt himself moving, not across geography any more, or even into himself so much as deeper into his Source.

During the journeys the inner action in him had been great. By now he had a guided, never a driven, but a settling sense that he was to point his life to the work at last. It was not easy for him, not when the world's versatility and enchantment, its legitimate joys of marriage and children, as well as the peaks of mindful attainments could have been his. Still, however easier to think it, but fate is not written, as a human you are free. You can choose to align yourself with what you know of your soul, or not.

Closer to Galilee, of a sudden he knew; the most intense communion with God's will was awaiting him. A confrontation in solitude, a decision about intent, a final weighing up. He had already forsaken the places and pleasures of men, forgone safety, the platforms of approval, acquisition, and honor. He had already left behind a lot. He would climb Mount Hermon alone, and in solitude chance losing the rest. But he would face his own mind, and live alone with the Lord Creator.

So back up North he went. Up, up, up into the mountainous world of panting brooks, of racing waters more than nine hundred feet high, a land of rock doves, pools of bur weed, and of the lagoons flanked by the groves of storax.

It was August. He spent the last three weeks of that infernal month and the first three weeks of a heat-numbed September on the mountain called Hermon.

When he came down from the mountain people stared. He was a silent, a much changed man. After Hermon his connection to the universe and to himself had altered. His preparation was complete.

The sharing could begin.

When he returned to Galilee's miracle-starved people he seemed to have stars and galaxies implied in him. To them he looked to have journeyed in many incarnations, known an infinity of lives. The seers of the land wanted to see him as their augury's fulfilment. The magicians and the mystics whispered, "He is the Avatar! The Solar Spirit! The One who is Coming."

But he was to stay a plain man, saying the most ordinary things, continually making himself be at one with others. He would be seen in places, a tallish white figure, speaking bow headed, sometimes in whispers, at other times, a man of humor, his hand held out or to his heart, a man walking and speaking on Palestine's earth.

Afterwards, when he was teaching, hardly anyone would recognize in this authoritative public man the younger man who had casually joked and chatted with them. Few could associate him with the carefree wanderer of the infectious muscular manner who had walked the world, light of tread and heart, with this consolidated man whose purity of intention shone out of him, his gravity of purpose framed by a veneration whose single point was God.

So great was the change in him.

After Mount Hermon his face had not so much altered, as assumed the form of finality. Also, as a human fashioned by the foods and weather and lights of a place, he now looked like that Hebrew land itself. If the vibrations of a place can be in a human, then he vibrated of that earth. He was very like his human home-world, for that one short time, the most favoured locale, yet so stone-average it could have been any battered old spot on earth. He resembled that country, looked integral to it, sun-seared, blond-streaked, powerfully veined and muscled, shot with light. His face was like that country's white light under which the Semitic mind had gone to One-ness, to the one-pointed apex of itself. But his voice was no longer crystal clarion as in youth. Its pitch had sunk to a texture like loam. Though level, its timbre had cracked on some nameless anguish, making it sound broken and soft. But it made people stop, look up. That lilting Galilean dialect of his speech now had authority. He had become possessed of self. No longer needing to watch for it, his bearing, both easy and centered anyhow, was even more natural. He had nothing deliberate about him, but a force of realism with a compassion so direct that it was felt to be from the Absolute itself. When he spoke in that hushed gritty voice, a centrality of spirit was in all he said. On listening to him, many a Jew struck himself on the breast, sensing, "Here it *is*—the completion of Jewish prayer!" His words were so much from who he was, and he, so at one with what he said, that no one could find in him the slightest divergence from the truth. He spoke, and it was truth, people felt, a man of full heart, his word transparent, and of God.

After Mount Hermon his home was never again to be Nazareth. Aside from old Zebedee, nobody knew where his travels had taken him. His own family of many siblings didn't even ask. Since it suited them, they believed he had only been to Alexandria. No one asking him directly about it, he neither confirmed nor denied it. Back at home he spent time with his mother. He, so silent with the goings-on inside him, Mary had to remark on it. But he couldn't answer her, or not very well, not the way she would have liked. So once again, his mother was bewildered—she was often that—always loving but never understanding him. Though Mary's mood had been shifting key. She was much closer to a blessing she never thought to have, less concern with the effects of her will on her son. Or indeed—and this was going to let Mary fly—on anything or anyone.

At this time of his most inexpressive silence, and to balance the immense inner mobilisation that would launch his public life, he went to build boats with old Zebedee, his father Joseph's friend. Concentrating on the interior crafting, the care of the small details of sea vessels, he stayed for a little in Galilee's gold quiet.

For Succoth he went up with old Zebedee to Jerusalem. The Feast of Tabernacles was at summer's torrid end. During this feast Israel's folk slept in tents of palms. Stars peeped in the roofs of foliage beneath which the

## His Real Life

people sang. Torch-lit processions of singing and wine, it was vacation time for the people. Among the circles of his friends on Jerusalem's hillsides, he joined in the singing of Succoth, the clapping of hands, the dancing hullabaloo of young and old.

Returning alone from Jerusalem, he was grateful to be trudging once more towards Capernaum by the sea. He saw again the fruits of citrus groves, the red soil, the marble houses, and the Hellenic synagogue looking out to that pearl drop of a sea. Galilee's was a huge panorama of burning white clouds shooting forth rays of many-spoked brilliance. A land of precious silence, he walked it, head bent, his top lip in a mute, meek curl of happiness as he passed the red flowers of a pomegranate. Under the blue sky he sensed the fragile beauty of the time left in which to be, to breathe the air, and just love God. Along the road he heard the jangle of stirrups and leather and saw the imperial purple of Caesar's legionaries and bade them the joy of the day. From their truculent steeds the soldiers looked down to see if he was just the usual rancid-tempered nation-mad Jew mocking them. And when they saw not, saw that he meant it, the soldiers laughed back a "Shalom! Shalom!" And not at all unpleasantly.

Back in Capernaum he put on his apron. He was keeping busy, a not much noted man again. How he relished his last moments of simplicity, a man robbed of breath at its unutterable beauty as he bent to a common lupin plant. By then he was very quiet. Nor was his the superior silence of the one-who-knew-everything but the quiet of the one entering the eye of the storm. As a craftsman at the Zebedee boat shop, he was known to be painstaking, focused on the over-all project, attentive to detail, though he wasted no time on trifles. In a land of iron-rigid custom in trade, as in everything else, he had hardly any personal rules, but one was, always work to your best. And he did. So he got a lot of satisfaction, also much praise. Though that did not much matter.

Time passed.

Rumors were reaching the Zebedee workshop in Galilee. They spoke of a John, a prophet, a man desert black. He, this John, he was a-coming, they said, calling Jews to the river Jordan, saying, "Turn! Come on! Get right with God."

The actual second Jesus heard this rumor, his head at a sharp tilt, eyes narrowed to a slit at measuring the fit of two planes, without one muscle shifting, his face lit up. This John, went the gossip, he was a rough, a hairy, a fiery man. He preached "Repent!," and, "Quit the unreality of sin!" As

*Ready*

John was heard to progress along the Jordan, thundering and baptising, he went on working, his heart slowly beating. He heard about John's rants, John's lashing at sin, his roars and blastings at wickedness. There was nothing much in him to say to that. But he knew; the moving of John along the river Jordan was the coming of his fate.

One day in a misty January, he was cobbling away at a rent on a boat's side, hammering in a nail. He had just looked down at the mallet, it reminding him of the garden mattock used by his mother Mary, she, such a fruitful grower of herbs, the delicious vegetables, especially the marrow spiced with the dill, when one of the workers pounded into the boat shop. John the prophet, spluttered this man, was baptising in nearby Pella. Jesus looked up. The winter air was an indeterminate gray. He looked through it mildly, the direction in him alerted.

And it all became clear.

He took off his apron. From a-midst of shaving wood, he, who never left a work unfinished, not even an untidied loose scrap, laid down all his tools. He folded his apron. "My hour" he said, "has come."

As he turned, a curl of wood lay on the bench.

*Chapter IX*

# John

John was split.

His mind split in the minute he and his cousin had met. One look at that face and all John's ideas were destroyed while his soul was shunted into a perfect, if still occluded consciousness.

Long before that visit, John's parents used to whisper and mutter about his cousin being the Messiah. As a youth, John shrugged at that. For everyone kept seeing Messiahs everywhere, so great was Israel's outrage, so wish-fraught the national sigh for deliverance.

Now, John had no nose for politics, no ear for history; he had no experience, no interest in cause and effect. All turned in him on a single point, as small as an atom and totally ungrasped, which John kept burying with apocalyptic bluster, but a point where John's true nature was waiting.

So when at eighteen John looked into the face of Jesus, he saw: This is not the face of the Jewish Messiah. Or the word 'Jewish' lost its meaning in a face like that. Or 'Messiah' had to be re-thought. But after that meeting, John kept the image of his cousin in him, but not from any conceit of Jesus being of his own blood-line, or that Jesus might enhance what John was about himself. No, indeed, for when he dared to bring his cousin's image forward, how *that* grew and how his own waned . . . No, but the impress of Jesus in John realigned his many turmoils into a healing and new, if quite incomprehensible, formation.

Returning home from the encounter, John tried telling himself, he'd only been struck because Jesus was more charming, a being more gracious than himself. True, Jesus was that happier kind, one to whom the best was likely, a man who made goodness seem easy and possible. But it was more than that. When John tried to gauge him, mentally walk around his cousin's qualities, he just couldn't. There were no sides, no top, no bottom-of-the-well in Jesus. He had no latitude. He was pure scope, all open, no closures, no end. Even the way he spoke, no jags of aggression in his words, no threat, no barbs, no hooks. He spoke, and it was straight, a transparent surface, the inside same as the outside. And it shone.

He boggled the mind of John.

A combustible, but clear thinker, this experience had embarrassed John. He spoke of it to no one of course. Nor did he have anyone to whom he could.

John of the desert had no schooling. He was a primitive—rigid, a man of no subtlety who took no count of either the sublime or animality in humans. Elizabeth and Zacharias, his elderly and virtuous parents, were from a priestly caste. By fourteen John had taken a religious vow in Engedi. It was the mediocre one of a Nazarite; to drink no intoxicants, to let the hair grow, and not touch the dead. These were the vows of the prophets Sampson and Samuel, meant to form a holy character. But the mettle in John was a-stir for a holiness more real than that. After that visit to Galilee, whenever his agitated mind landed on his cousin, John knew; he was getting closer to what holiness was.

When Zacharias died John went on caring for his mother and tending the sheep in that inferno of a shadeless Beersheba. Ferociously principled, he refused the funds due to him as a Nazarite. So he and his mother were very poor. His contact with the world remained sparse. While grazing his herd on the desert's lean grasses, John read, but only Jewish Scripture. His hair was raggy; it flew about, snaky at the ends, long down his back. He had taken the style of Elijah for his own, and wore a kind of hairy dress. John was tall, more than six feet, a streak of black lightning in the white desert sun. He had a mission and it was nameless, so he suffered, not knowing what it was.

Being who he was, John could have lived under the pressure of the ineffable forever in the wilderness, had the world of Jewish tumult not asserted itself.

Hundreds of years of agony—that was how the children of Abraham felt. Bondage to Rome, they believed, was the cause of it. The Hebrew Semites suffered more horribly than anyone from Rome's incursion on them.

Humiliated by Rome's secular Imperium, they were outraged by its conquest, its taxes, its foreign disrespect. To a people who experienced their race as the seat of their identity, their suffering was worse. And should a prophet say to them, 'Forget about race, go beyond it. It's not what you are; your race is not your identity,' why, such a one had to be the Devil, the enemy!

The Romans scoffed at the Hebrews' God. To Rome it was just Jewish self-infatuation. For long had the Caesars declared the Jew not fit to live, since the Jew did not love humanity. Did the *Yehudim* themselves not say, "We are the chosen of God?" But where was the proof of that? Weren't they just feeling whipped to the bone? So the questions boiling out of Jewish humiliation were: Why? and How can we, the chosen nation, re-assert ourselves?

"Repent!" was the apocalyptic reply. "Repent, and God will send the Messiah who will return us to the throne of power." "And," some added, "to the whole world this time."

Reared on rumors of his kinsman being this kind of Messiah, when John actually met him in that Nazareth yard among the chickens, the goats, and the odd few rats, his cousin was nothing like that. Jesus was gentle. No pomp-addled and gristly Lord of power, he was a smiler, blond-streaked, a gold skinned boy prone to laugh and jest with his brothers. To John he seemed as meek as a girl, his nature sacrificial rather than assertive, and, John recalled, he was actually very funny at times. If Jesus was ever powerful and right, it was only in passing, he didn't *mean* to—he just was.

Nevertheless, to John who did not understand the world, the politics of the times were boding the end. To his ponderings, as he sat among his herd of animals, it seemed the end of an age. From his pious Scripture-reading, like other earnest myopics, John looked out blind over the backs of his grazing flock into the flat white light of Beersheba, and saw; it was beginning! The Age of God! In a single zealous swipe he swept all doubt aside and went to live a prophet's life, (not unusual for the times) to preach "Repent! Get right with God! Get ready for the end! The Kingdom of Heaven is at hand!"

Still, the more he preached "The End" to people, the more confused John became. From his meeting of Jesus years back, another order, not of an apocalypse, had taken root in him. For all his railings at sinners, John sensed a message in Jesus radically different from his. If Jewry dreamt of being freed from Rome, Jesus had dreamt of quite another deliverance. So, if the truths of Jesus contradicted his own, then, John had to ask, what were his own thunderings about? What was *his* purpose then?

He prayed on this. How humbly he, a proud and fervid Jew prayed for guidance! But to his years of prayer no light would come. He went on baptizing up and down the Jordan, but inwardly becoming more and more numb. Yet, John's followers just about adored him. People loved him for his passion, for nobility and naturalness. But what did John care? Split about his purpose, there were times he could hardly feel himself as alive, rather as a man held back and apart. And his preaching, "Repent!" grew steadily more obsolete to his soul, the "Sin," and the "Be Saved," less and less important. John cared nothing for acclaim. He got no profit, not a shred of gain from it. He had no sense of his own worth, of his own warmth, or courage—none. And though by now John's entire desert vision of doom and judgment felt irrelevant, he went on preaching, a hoarse man of cracked voice, a shell, a hole. He lived hollow, a thing carved out, waiting only to be filled. But by whom? By One, John knew, in at least the few salved moments of his proofless existence, by the One who was coming.

One day in Adamon, thousands of pilgrims on the Jordan, and a graying old woman tugging at his bare arm, asked, "Are you the Messiah?"

John turned to her. And like a bird, it just flew out of him, the ease of the reply, "There is one to come after me who is greater than I, whose sandal I am not worthy to loosen. I baptize you with water. But he shall baptize you with the fire of the Spirit."

Though afterwards, glum in his lone tent, he didn't know what he had meant. Nor was there ever a moment he thought to link the One he was to point the way for, with Jesus, the son of Joseph.

Not, that is, until he came to John.

One January day near Pella, John had been baptizing in the Jordan. It was nearly noon. And he was tired. He had been shriveling all morning, his skin turning wrinkly in the water. More than a hundred still in line, the people on the bank were moaning and wailing as usual to him. Exhausted, John looked up. Out over the river he saw two of his cousins, Jude and James of Nazareth. And companionably standing with them, their brother, Jesus. The sight of him, apart from being rugged in a workmanish way, there was nothing special about it. But John, shin deep in the water, went light in the head. Ecstasy, when it came at last, John being so lean of soul he couldn't experience it in his senses, except perhaps as a rush of truth. He turned a blind circle on his own axis in the water, his face blank. But in the desert of his mind John knew—what had always been coming to him, was come.

Jesus was coming down the line, down with the people, down the river bank. He was talking in a friendly way to the women and the men on the line, nodding his head, listening in that deep smiley way he had. And then he was there before John in the water, bare shouldered, a man full of grace. John looked at him, a stainless man, himself as if underwater, numb.

"Why," he mouthed "why do you come to me?"

"To be baptized by you."

"But it is I, who need to be baptized by you."

"Bear with me," the tone of Jesus was unimportant, "to set an example to my brothers standing here with me. And as a sign that my hour has come."

John had known the whole of this, though with no understanding that he had. Now he simply bent to the water. And taking them into his arms, he baptized in the Jordan the brothers Jude and James.

When it came to Jesus, the four men in the muddy green water heard a sound above. Never having heard anything like that, they couldn't have said what it was. As Jesus bent for the water, a voice issued a clear sense into them all, "This is my beloved Son in whom I am well pleased."

Nothing much was happening on the Jordan. People were looking on from afar. A crow croaked in the wintry sky. Jesus was slightly bowed. His head was lowered as he took it in, this final sealing of his task. Hands lightly placed across his chest, he received his identity's vocation, obediently took its confirmation, there in the water between sky and ground. He accepted from the Father who he was, and all that was to come.

Now the way was open.

On the Jordan a midday silence sat. The water stayed level, not a ripple. The reeds on the bank did not stir, nor the clear cool trees of winter. Even the clattery palms were still, submerged in the sky's blue spatial sleep. Nothing moved. But the face of Jesus turning skyward shifted planes, absorbing truth. And when he next looked down on the river again Jesus was changed.

His brothers stood by as he wrapped the outer garment about himself. He bent to the ground, re-tied his sandals, and set out for the hills of Perea where, in solitude for forty days, he would enter himself. Pushing the curious, pestering people aside, John was hobbling behind Jesus, but staying back and to the side, wordless thing that happened, and was now past. Jesus

*John*

walked out of the water, re-wrapped his mantle, his himself now tapering, vanishing, clarified. To the back of Jesus, John was shouting snatches of a legend, "Before your birth, your mother had been visited by the angel of the universe."

Jesus heard. But with no expression, he kept going ahead.

"The angel" called John, "told Mary you will be the Soul-Healer. I now know you are he," John fell back as Jesus went forward, "and who I am."

John the Baptizer went back south after that. His personality, having fulfilled its function, was at its end. He was finished. And deep inside John knew it.

Still, he went on preaching just a little while more.

And so, after a short life of inept moralism, a new tenderness began in John. He felt it was just perfect, that the one for whom he had lived had always been known to his soul. John's words to people came to be about God's mercy. He no longer berated the Pharisee "vipers." He no longer thrashed sin, or augured judgment, fire, woe, or revenge. Though his verbal assaults on public corruption remained incorrigible. Swinging into full momentum, he turned on that generally acknowledged swine, Herod Antipas for the immorality of taking another man's wife. So Herod, who both admired and feared John, threw him into prison at the fortress of Machaerus in Perea. John's disciples scattered, some of them going to join Jesus.

John's prison. Darkness. Cold. Stone. Loneliness. But none of these daunted him too much. He longed for only the one thing—to see Jesus. To hear one word, just the one sign. In a year and a half of deprivation John's sturdy frame shrunk to a crabbed and filthy scarecrow's with the lack of nearly all that made for life. He was given hardly any food, almost no water. He could not clean himself. At times in the fetid dungeon there was no air. In the stinging cold, then the stuporous heat he was tormented by doubt. Yet in some small place in him, John knew the most burning joy imaginable. He, an empty man, had been filled. Once a man of too many words, now in the silence he saw, Jesus, a man, was the Word. Up till then John only knew the half of a perfect equation, which went, "This universe is a thought God had." In prison he was to close the gap, "Jesus is God's word to Man." And knowing such things in the squalor of prison John's heart stayed a-wing in slow ecstasy, while his body was speedily wracked in torture.

Later, hearing of his cousin's growing fame and tremendous effect, John merely repeated to those who still visited him, "He must increase, but

## His Real Life

I must decrease. I have said my portion. But He, of Heaven, has come to say the word of God."

But not a word was sent to him in prison. Not one. None of his kinsman's power or influence was exercised for John. So the feat of John was to be this; to not be crushed by disappointment that Jesus did not come to see him.

When, in the end, his anguish became humanly unbearable, John had to send word to Jesus. With the most sublime restraint this was all he asked, "Is my work done?"

This time a messenger did come back. Jesus had said, "Tell John, the poor have the good tidings preached to them. Say to John, he is the beloved herald of my mission and to not stumble over me, but be blessed in the ages to come."

This was the last word from Jesus to John, who thought this answer to his question was divine, divinely enough, enough and divine.

A few days later, to keep a promise made in a drunken hour to Salome, a girl hardly thirteen and already lost, Herod beheaded John.

*Chapter X*

# Baptism and Forty Days

That day by the Jordan stood the world's most humiliated people. The children of Israel were hurt. Jews lived in a weeping mortification by their lot. Sin, they believed, was their misery's cause. Between the zinc-blue mountains of Judea and the hills of Perea John the Baptizer had bawled to the nation, "Repent!" And people had; they took the baptism of John to wash away sin. For, were Israel's sins flushed away by animal blood, or with water, as John more moderately did, the Lord would renew to his chosen ones, his lapsed, covenantal blessing.

The Hebrew nation was in a welter of longing. Its people were viced in pain. The Jews were, as they kept repeating to themselves via Scripture, a special people. The received story of the Semitic nomads who crossed the Jordan, marched into Canaan and slaughtered its inhabitants was that Yahweh, the Lord of All, told them to do it.

Thus, on Rome's take-over of land, the Hebrew paroxysm of anguish at having the nation's property taken away. Long tutored into feeling as a "we," Jews lived in a howl of wrath that their nation, their identity itself, was in foreigners' hands. They had to have it back. Their existence as Jews hung on it. Because, to be Jews had been God's Command. So the God who told you to be a people, to pray together, and to repent, would also be a God to call you together for collective acts of claim and revenge. Thus had boiled out of the centuries of insult and seething, the need for a Messiah to restore God's realm.

So was it that Rome's conquest of their land was felt to be more of a rape for the Hebrews than for other peoples. They longed for a national figure to deliver them. Nor was this deliverer to be any spiritual envoy of the Divine, but a restorer of territory, of geographic and power losses, and this would be justice on earth.

At the time of the baptism of Jesus, this yearning for the old Davidic glory had reappeared as race penitence to usher in the Messiah.

But when Jesus of Nazareth stood in the Jordan, it was not in penitence for sin. It was not for any messianic dream of land-and-power restoration. He stood in line with others out of piety, just to be with them. The inner meaning of John's baptism was a symbolic act, to identify the whole of life with the Creator's purposes. This was the deep consecrational streak in John. Baptism meant a lot to Jesus. It was why he had come. Nor, when he went under the water was it to remit sin, or rekindle God's lapsed favor to the nation. It was to offer his life-work to the Father, a Son-of-God act. Jesus was sinless; anyone could see it, as may be any woman or man. To show this was why he had not come alone to be baptized, but deliberately with his brothers. His body's going under the water was his soul's offering itself, a giving over of all intention and future purposes. The instant he joined his will to God's, Jesus fused with the God-spirit resident in himself. He went into it, and was met by it, fusing as he stood in the water between earth and sky. As his soul met God's spirit, it united with the personality of the man in the water, the Jew, Yeshua ben Joseph.

Now he was one with it.

From then on Jesus was to be in a continuous contact with total reality, the natural outcome of a soul having joined the spirit of the Father. In the exaltation of it, he prayed the simple human words he had, "Father in heaven; Hallowed be thy name. Your kingdom come. Your will be done..."

Now the man in the shallow green river turned. As, eyes open, he stood in the water, slightly bent, Jesus sustained a glimpse of the indescribable—God's unlimited spirit bathing all creation. And from that, because Paradise *does* impact on matter, he saw the work to be done here.

Knee deep in the Jordan's brown water, the time he had taken to encompass the vision of all this, he was thirty one and a half years of age, a totally offered up man, having achieved at soul all that a person of his generation humanly can.

When he came out of the water that day, for the first time, it was clear to him. Humanly though, his body shook. He was trembling at what he now knew. He shivered as he waded back to shore. Jesus shook because his mind had been entered by a total clarity. What he would make of the knowledge received, how he would endure it and act to it, was to be the story of the rest of his existence. But to the people on the bank he was only trembling at the not unusual coolness of late winter.

He had now to be alone. He had to adjust to it. He had to integrate who he was with what the work of it implied. Until this event (so celestial in one aspect, so ordinary in another) Jesus didn't fully know his personal status or function. Like everyone he had to grow to it, to earn it.

The year Yeshua ben Joseph walked out to the Perean hills to be alone with the will of God was the year Augustus Caesar died, and Tiberius, co-Emperor with Augustus for fifteen years, became sole Caesar of Rome, and also the year Pontius Pilate, a mediocre man to be remembered for nothing but the one abysmal bungle, began as Governor of Judea.

Leaving John by the Jordan, Jesus began to stride out. He lunged out toward the Perean hills. He had now to pay mind to the plans in him taking shape. That Perean wilderness was not an empty desert, but gently lived in by a few meek animals, birds, scrub, lean grasses, some water. Nor was the encounter of Jesus out there with a roaring, snorting, reptilian Satan; it was with a being of his own calibre, a personality-form visible in a dimension always potentially on offer, but now having accepted his status, fully available to him. The being Jesus met out there on the hills was Gabriel, the universe's first executive.

Since the fusion of Jesus with God's spirit, Gabriel had some universe information for him; the earth-task of Jesus was actually finished. His world-work was done. He now had full moral consciousness. His attainment lay in experiential completion at the right hand of the Father. He, Jesus, a Creator Son, could claim that place at any moment he chose.

But he remained out there, absorbing all this. Time went by, and he wasn't really surprised, for he knew there had always been this chance. And he was discovering it now, a personal gap, a reluctance to leave, even now when it was the end. He would allow himself forty days to decide what to do with it. Indeed, given Gabriel's brief to him, the questions already started, was anything more required of him? For instance, at this moment of summation, why not leave this world, return to glory?

The truth was, in the living of this life and his own nature, he felt a tremendous ardor to do something for this world, an ardor, a desire stronger than the outspread arms of heaven's welcome itself. But he did not humanly know what. The proposal to him was, "Stay here and affirm by your presence the holiness of the creation." So the dilemma was this: Could he endure further separation from God in this hiatus (a relative torment!) of space-time? Could he stay with earth?

On the thin-soiled ground of Perea he brought himself to the first decision; no, he would not leave humans. He would continue with them. But out here in the wilderness he was warring with no hissing devils; what he faced was far worse, a division of loves in the heart. His split about this first decision was of a lover's equal aching for the worst and the best—and on this perverse planet of paradox and pathos, sometimes the worst *was* the best! But he would stay on with this world, rough and infirm as it was.

So yes, he would abide.

Next came the question of how to live. By now all material power was his. Now that he knew how power worked all was at his behest. To his mind was now unfurled the most mind-stretching of relationships, full access to the mechanisms of matter, and also to the personnel who administered the universe. "But," he warned himself, "resort to no power not humanly mine." So the second decision was made; to live as a human among others.

During his hill wanderings in Perea, Jesus did not fast. His water intake was minimal. He went after the edibles to be had on the land and was grateful to find some. He took enough of food to sustain his senses, so that truth be not invented by his condition but grow manifest to it. Out there on Perea's hillsides the days were hot and still. Or he was making himself be still in them. Time here, as everywhere, was not magically neutralized, or mystically irrelevant, but of a precise sequence and consideration. Dawns and dusks, they came and went; time beat on by and he still refused to fast, rejecting such egoic body-mind tactics as a way to God. By day he walked about slowly. At night he found a cave and slept in it. Come mornings, and despite the renewing stress of decisions to be made, he felt blessed, at one with the peace of mineral-blue hills, the "peep!" of birds, the insect life of the air and of the ground. Alert to the confluence of his human and divine mind, his time among Perea's savage rocks and tender rivulets were the first days of the two minds being made one.

Next, Gabriel reminded him of the two ways he could go. Both ways were good. To both routes he had full right. His was the Creator choice. His own course would prove excellent for himself: the other path was to fulfil the creature life projected for him by the Trinity of Paradise.

## Baptism and Forty Days

Once more, as on Mount Hermon, he was halted by that split. How could the two ways, his own and God's, conflict? How could living truly for the One, and living truly for the All ever be at loggerheads? If his intention was good, did the One and the All not flow into each other no matter at what point he entered? How could his own way not be the same as the ideal projected for him by Paradise?

It was impossible.

But then, slowly, he was seeing it. They were not at odds. One did not negate the other. But the one was the more capacious love. A life lived for all would serve as a paradigm, not just for his own worlds, but for all the Universes of the Paradise Father.

During this time he lived in a rock shelter near the village of Beth Adis. He drank from springs, ate berries and tubers, the birds he caught. Under a greenish sky at evening he would stand quite still, sifting, sorting, not driven mad by not yet knowing. There were times though he did feel weak. Then he lay down in the wilderness, his face to the ground, feeling in these times, the approach of some terribleness.

Because next, a serious matter, already an issue, and to become a problem—Time. The spirit in him did not operate in time, had no time-consciousness. So his soul, already fused with spirit knew, in a personality of his order, any desire not conflicting with God's would automatically manifest. His own creative energy was so aligned to universe force that his will directly impacted upon reality. This caused matter to immediately conform itself to any desire of his, consistent with the Universal will. "For God's sake," he warned himself sternly and again, "Don't ever lose time-consciousness!" Because the appearance of any wish in a Creator Son meant its instant enactment!

His fourth decision concerned food, that metaphor for the many hungers of humanity. As on Mount Hermon, so now too, how he wished for all the Sonship to be fed! But he decided, "Tread the ordinary road to bread. Do everything the way it is done on earth."

By now really hungry himself, he was quite thin. He looked lean and rangy, but not to the point of danger. The question of bread was raising the issue of gratification; why did people believe that living in your senses led to happiness?

Historically the times were bursting into materiality and surface, throwing up the sensualities of emotion and sex, of body decoration, mystic rituals, sensitivities, obsessions and fixations, fetishes with food and appearance. But if the most noble of the pagan vision was a dream for a lover with whom to extinguish yourself, then the reality he had on offer was a joy more thorough than that. It was to forget about your sense perceptions and the rage-soaked judgments based upon them, to engage with the adventure of a friendly universe and attain its full range right up to God. Life was surely a living out your own choices and their expression, a fate more fitting for humans with no extinction. For, didn't the pleasure of the struggle for the ideal by far out-weigh the satiation of the life preserving urges? As Scripture said, "Man shall not live by bread alone but by every word of God . . ."

So, no, he wouldn't live for bread. Bread was not what man was made for. Bread was not enough. Nor would he use his talents for glory and fame. Though you shouldn't give up your talents out of fear of failure, either.

Up before dawn, he found himself close to a precipice. He leaned over, stared down, and an abyss yawned under him. It flung up the question: what to do in situations of danger? Should he provide the net of a miracle? Re-arrange matter to save himself? No, he decided, just take normal human care. He would not lean on heaven, nor defy nature, the manifest law of the Father's present will.

In those ages out on the plains, his blood ran low. These were the times he found his human mind doubting the divine mind. In matters like this, he couldn't have not doubted. Doubt was one of the conditions of being on earth. As a man, it remained with Jesus, the full gamut of the human, its duality and divisiveness. And the human in him was doubting the affirmation of the divine. He had the natural urge for veracity. He was strict with objections, on guard to the fantastical. So, tormented by it, he now asked, "Could the divine mind do something for the human mind to help it subdue its doubt? Just the one thing? Or was forcing a superhuman assurance against the will of the Father?"

He sat on the ground, watchful. His heart at a low ebb. He sat there, scrawny by now, gone vague and cloudy under a featureless sky. He looked out, his mind dulled. In the thin shade of a meagre tree, against the inertia of doubt he made himself call to mind God's spirit. "Trust it," he decided with the energy left. "Life is proof enough of divinity. So yes." He consented to the smallness of it, making himself content, if not with proof replete, with what was. And this was enough.

*Baptism and Forty Days*

Still later, and still blank under a cement winter sky, he thought of his own Israelites and found himself fantastically longing for them. He wished to have some affect on Jewry's heart, always on the brink of spirit and matter. To speak to his people was the most urgent human desire Jesus ever had. But if he did not perform miracles, they would not believe in him. Of course he knew the short-cuts to effects. He had travelled, learnt, had made wide contact, knew the methods with matter and the affairs of men, knew how to win and stun. Since he knew the techniques of power he could have cut through the established processes; he could have mesmerized the nation, walked on air, or on water before the entire world. And won it. But how would gagging displays of a magician put the love of God in hearts? And yet, might he not soothe his own heart by winning over Israel's in just one single display of the dominion they craved as proof of their Messiah?

No, he decided. He would not lift so much as a finger to legitimize himself. People could accept what he said on trust, see the truth of it, have faith in it, or not. He would do no miracles to prove his authority, his credentials not being the point. Nor would he use his virtually unlimited power to breach nature. It would only over-awe them. Nor would he use the energy of the divine to fuel his people's national fever.

So, no miracle, no favoritism for any sect. But what of the grand total of humanity? Might not each and every one of his planetary loved ones be shifted to glory by the one single, world-stuporating performance from his hand? Couldn't the global good be conjured, like, snap! by one single, irresistible sweep of stunning authority, instead of the slow, painful, step-by-step choice-discovery of each individual? Was he to decline all power? Achieve all by slow human work and will?

His own way would be swift, instant, spectacular, intense; the way of the Father's was less focused on any one world, but distributed in gain to all. The choice was re-presented to him; the good of the One? Or the good of the All? The first was dramatic, immediate, vivid; the second was distant, lumbering, age-slow. The slowness of God's way might be, humanly speaking, a bitter cup. Even so; he decided to drink it.

Very thin now and bowed to the ground, he was seared by hunger, slowed-down, frustrated, held back. But worse, he grieved to be declining those conquests symbolized by "The Throne of David." He, an earthborn Jew, was his people's grand and even possibly last, chance to achieve a supra-national eminence. He was the fulfilment of Israel's mission to be a torch-bearer of God to the world. But then, really loving them, he would not use the power of God in him for something tragically less in the end—the restoration of Israel's temporal power. For an instant before him Jesus saw it—earth's humanity so quickened by miracle that they could more easily find God. But was it his to wrest the course of evolution from humanity's hand? His brief was single. His mission, as slow as Paradise, to bring by grace, and not by power, the Father God to the world.

Forty days, and he was ending his struggle with choice. He said "No" to all racial honor. He bade farewell to all the messianic references urged on him by his mother and friends. Mentally he let go of his childhood's loved guides, each nudging him to be a prophet, a hero, Salvatore of their nation. In one clear sweep Jesus made an end in himself of the nostalgia of Jewish expectancy, cutting clear from all racial longings, all miasmas, bogs for the spirit.

Of these forty days and nights of solitude he was making a good human end. But he didn't know the next step. Still, the brunt of the decision had been borne; he refused the use of spiritual power for temporal ends. All this for the achievable, if long-distance, good.

He would go back. Back to the Galilee, always to remain for him that light-in-the-rose place. He would begin the work there. To those who would hear, he would speak of God. This was all. It would be as small as that. His task in the end was simple, to be done and said. To turn to God's spirit, walk life's way, one step after another.

In rejecting messianic power Jesus knew he had almost certainly secured his people's religious rejection. His placing of the individual over the interests of the nation would be almost a treachery; his valuing of soul over the ideal of community would be heard as blasphemy. To speak of "soul" at all to that collective social order would be received as a death blow to it.

As he turned back towards the Jordan, that river of transformation, grief for his people ransacked Jesus. Nonetheless, he made the one last concrete resolution; he would do all to stop people from seeing him as Messiah. They would have only a nationalistic concept of that. Not until they understood the spiritual meaning of that word did he wish for it to be used.

Still, with sorrow he knew: in all his doings and acts he would be stormed everywhere in that needy, clingy, squalling and battering world by three vociferations, all impatiences of the spirit.

First, they would insist on miracles.

Second, they would always demand to be fed.

And the final failure of comprehension would be the desire to turn him into a mascot of their nation, to make him King of the Jews.

*Chapter XI*

# His Friends

A lmost everyone knew him by then.
When after forty days he strode out of the Perean hills and ploughed back in among the throngs of John's followers—thousands of the God-throng still camped at Pella—there was hardly a soul there who had not heard of him.

### Andrew

The man Andrew, was one of these. An innocent of placid faith, Andrew was taciturn, stank of fish, a boyish man, dogged and good. A follower of the Baptist, Andrew had been in that crowd somewhere at that baptism on the Jordan's bank. Though when he first saw Jesus arriving with his brothers arm in arm, and heard a few things he said, Andrew no longer felt too serene any more. On hearing the words of the man, a trap door opened in Andrew, and he fell, he didn't know where. Once a man to be impatient with because of his rather pat idealism, Andrew woke up with a jolt. And while Jesus was gone roaming Perea, Andrew waited by the Jordan; he didn't know why.

Later, outside his tent, he heard the Baptist muttering, "He is the world's light."

When he returned from his days out in the land Jesus ploughed back into that waiting crowd. Mingling with the people again, he bumped shoulders with Andrew in the crowd. As they chanced to look eye to eye for a second, Andrew heard his own throat catch. After the man's days in the hills, Andrew was stunned by the physical change in him. But did recall, yes, of course he had met him—wasn't he the boat maker at Zebedee's of Capernaum? But what a change! Andrew had never seen a face of such practical cheer, the real holiness of a man. At this time of Israel's cry for prophets to deliver them, Andrew, a pious man, walked up to Jesus.

"Master," he asked, "I would follow you."

Jesus opened his arms. He embraced the man. This was apostle number one. Andrew was the first man chosen, a human moved by the sheer presence of Jesus to follow him.

As that consensus of people spontaneously addressed Jesus "Master," so, with a twist of humor added, Andrew was dubbed "Chief." He was the ablest of men. He could spot hidden resources even in the very young. He was a good man, never jealous of even that superseding brother of his, the much more exciting Simon. Andrew was oldish, reticent, a shaggy, wrinkled-over man. He had no dramatic persona, kept himself at a low-pitch, in a minor-key key out of humility for God. He was never annoyed at being put second, or indeed, last. His weak point was he held back on delight. Andrew was most touched by the friendliness of Jesus. A question he was to never answer was; "How could such a man live so close to God and be *so* considerate of humans?" Andrew only *just* missed waking up to the causal link between friendliness and Godliness. But he was always to be intrigued by it in Jesus.

In that extreme world that doled out death for what you said, the apostle Andrew, a physically robust man would take two days to die, crucified in Patra, Achaea.

## SIMON PETER

When Jesus gave Simon the nickname of "Peter," it was with the tenderest of smiles for the much ado about this man. Peter was a hot-head. A feeling would strike him and he would trumpet it about. Afterwards he might duck and splutter, playing the ingénue or the wag, but really, he just liked the drama of himself, to over-feel and rush at things. Though his self-enjoying bombast out-roared and up-staged Andrew's muffled mien, Simon deeply respected his older brother. He was burly-hearted, foolish and frank. But he had the gift of the gab and spoke very well.

When in Perea he asked the Master if he could join him also, Jesus looked Simon, an almost irresistible person, in the eye. "Your enthusiasm is your strength," Jesus couldn't stop smiling, his eyebrows helplessly opening at the gutsy appeal of the man, "But it's also a danger. In the work we are to do, we will speak of the heart, a realm, Simon, requiring the gentlest of tact. Would you just think before you speak? Can you do that? Maybe," he ribbed the big chap, "we'll find a name for you, something steady—how about, Peter, the rock?"

Simon's lips pouted. "Hmm, all right. Yes!" His self-esteem a bit nicked, but still, he liked the sound of it. Peter was physically huge, quick to act. A rough diamond, what he most liked in Jesus was the quality of refined tenderness. Peter swung from extreme to extreme, his faults being of the head, not of the heart. Though an exuberant egoist, when he first saw Jesus, he instantly grasped, if not the full girth, the gist of the man. But he hid his ecstasy. And played at being amused at the nickname he had been granted. He hid it, because when he dared to look at the image of Jesus found in his heart, it was of the best person who lived in it. Turning to that image as to a mirror (the only way Peter could look at Jesus, otherwise, as in the myth, if you looked directly at the divine you'd go blind,) he saw in it the full range of everything he loved. The very thought of Jesus made Peter want to shout and jump. So he hardly ever indulged that look-in.

Feeling half mad with it at times, Peter went to his life-mate, Perpetua. His wife said, "What to make of an obsession, my Peter, is what you do with it. If it drives you nuts," she, a roly-poly earth-mother, laughed, "well, that's all right, so long as you don't do nutty things!"

And what had his love for Jesus made Peter do so far? It did for Peter what it would for every one; Jesus increased the active area of soul in each person. Meeting Jesus let each person leave a broader trail of actualized reality in the world. And the love he felt for Jesus also let Peter know adoration for the first time. Love let Peter be first to grasp the divinity in the humanity of the man—even if also the first to deny him.

Vocal and rash, Peter was to be a powerful preacher. Only toward the end of his life would he revert to an aberrant ploy of Jesus being the Jewish Messiah. Too keen to win Jews as converts, Peter would lapse to spreading Jesus as their racial deliverer, a redeemer from sin, an untruth to con no Jew at all, and at odds with Jesus being a revealer of the Father for all.

Peter ended considering himself too honored to die the same way as his Master had; he asked to be inverted in his death. He was crucified head down in Rome, which, more than any other city since then, has identified itself with Peter.

Also by that baptismal river Jordan were the sons of Zebedee, James and John. Having worked with Jesus on the Lake, they were already his best of friends. From the day he swung into their patriarch's compound whistling under his breath, they liked him. There was also David, their wild-blood of an older brother, a man impatient with the noise made by religion, yet at least as much a friend of Jesus as themselves. Also on pilgrimage at Pella, the two younger Zebedees had taken upon themselves to go out searching for Jesus in the hills for days. When after their hectic hunt, they saw Andrew and Peter already in company with him, the Zebedee two, proud, bumptious boys, were dismayed; others had been preferred! Others were the first with Jesus!

The brothers Zebedee were making the mournful lowing cattle noises of the missed-out.

"But you were already with me before the others." laughing, Jesus chided them, "in my heart, I always counted you as in the kingdom. And you might have also been numerically the first, but you were off on self-appointed tasks. Why did you seek me? I was not lost. So look, my friends," he whacked each one on the back, "give no mind to who is first or last! Only to the doing of Heaven."

The Zebedees took this biff-on-the-chin in good grace.

Particularly young John.

## John Zebedee

An uncannily good looking boy, John wasn't exactly attractive, but cut off from others by the handicap of his own extreme comeliness. The lyrical looks, his ample blond hair, a lovely youth's face, had early isolated him. Particularly women were devoted to the handsome young John. Nor did this lavishing by the slavish make John's life easy. For was it a favor to be so adulated, when, as his withdrawal was proving, it was John who needed to get out of himself and love? This youngest of the Zebedees was to remain single all his life. Much later in old age, and only in conformity with custom, he married his brother's widow. But John of the almost disastrous beauty was never able to love.

Not, that is, except him.

When he first saw the carpenter from Nazareth saunter into their workshop, a rugged man more than ten years older, and an infinity more than that, young John experienced a flash—he had just been drubbing a plank of wood but at the sight of Jesus, he dropped it, on a surge of total human magnificence. The event for John was of being pierced by adoration, a tide of bliss, followed thankfully by its prudent withdrawal. A reflex of survival let John leisurely bend, replace the plank correctly, smile, though a little too primly, then turn and go. He left the workplace while Jesus was still absorbed in the meeting of those who worked there. John stepped away languidly from the shed, then, once around the corner, tore like mad, his face as he ran, burning through what felt like an avalanche.

In the following year of his being taken over, John had more than a few soul-flashes like that. While working on the boats with Jesus, and, too conceited to show it, John skulked behind the others, ear pricked for every word Jesus said. John knew, whatever his own games were, his attention had been arrested by the two maximals of Jesus, God and Man. John was basically jejune, narcissistic, a concealing, dreamy boy. But as the character of Jesus became his focus, his labor and nature improved. He started arriving to work the same time as others. His facial expression grew less wafty, his verbal expression more tangible. As he let himself be more inwardly grasped, even a few of John's fancies became graspable. He always wanted to be with Jesus. In his company John felt there would come a time when he was going to be a more useful person, more himself, more workable.

Of the apostles, John was the youngest, to Jesus most dear, but definitely not "the disciple Jesus loved"—a dotty thing John fell to burbling in a self-absorbed old age. He was a chum of Jesus, a close friend, but not a whit more favored than the others. John turned out to be prompt and utterly loyal "unto blood" if needed. He had the steely courage that sometimes goes with the conceitedness of the creatively imaginative, and he would be the only one well-nerved enough to follow Jesus right through his arrest and to the cross. Indulged as a child by fawning, submissive women, John grew up with no idea of, or any practice of, love. What woke him up was the love in Jesus. When he understood it, John became devoted to love as the virtue on which all the others were based. An aged preacher in Ephesus, he was to always farewell his flock with, "My little children, love one another."

The early death of his brother James took the "thunder" out of John. In later years he was to learn how a "soft answer turns away wrath." No longer pugnacious, and for all his acquired civility, John was exiled to the Greek isle of Patmos, a rocky outcrop of apocalyptic aspect in the Aegean. Here John wrote the Book of Revelations, a work bunglingly edited, distorted, and now in a dysfunctional form of itself.

He died after the longest time, aged a hundred and one, still astonished by love, in Ephesus.

### JAMES ZEBEDEE

He was a compressed sort of man. James and his brother John were nicknamed by Jesus "Sons of Thunder" for being a pair of head-strong, blustering men. As in others, anger in James was a form of condemnation. But when he met Jesus, James saw straightaway, he had no right to judge anyone. After that decision to swallow himself, there was a shift as James went on developing to depths more real than his railing old spit-and-spat, punchy self.

James was analytical, the one best able to see what Jesus meant. He observed people come to their best in his presence. He saw Jesus evoke beauty from men, focus and capacity from women, laughter from children, renewal in the sad, and from the old, benevolence. James was a fisherman on Lake Gennesaret, and personally much moved by the beauty of the lake region. He liked the rings of folded land, the aquatic birds of that small sea, the gulls, the cormorants, the plovers, the whole of that donkey-brown, calf-bleating, cock-crowing Galilean earth. He was also the type to ponder matters such as the universal laws he was learning from Jesus. A question that held him was if Paradise is not a material place, how could the physical universes be patterned on it? And another, if Paradise was God-as-matter, and the Infinite Spirit was God-as-mind, then—James was to complete this sequence before anyone—the Son was God-as-person, God as relationship.

For all his lucidities, James was often depressed. He would sink into brooding silences. Still, he got on well with his brother, though John could be as abstruse and self-contained as an egg. James was a natural planner, crisp and focal, the antidote for a loose cannon like Peter. As the Zebedee boys matured, the "Sons of Thunder" tag came to apply in its transfigured meaning to them. Just as, from languid and vague, John grew to be an intense enthusiast of love, so James became a true "Son of Thunder" by how the passion for service grew in his life. In maturity James became a daily server, a person who worked and sought no reward. His work's motive outgrew the law of credit-for-merit. Result and success were replaced in him by the values of obedience. The olden prophets had thundered of the pay-out for performance; but Jesus commended the doing of virtue not because it works, or gets results, but for itself, because it was good. Thus was James able to stand the ethic of "outcome" on its head by working out of fidelity to God alone. This new value personalized his daily acts, enduing them with an authority beyond the pressure for results. It freed James to be in a personal relation to the source of his motivation.

When his convictions were challenged, James spoke bravely. He had no eye for approval or assent. He was the first to be put to the sword under the rule of Herod Agrippa. The manner in which James Zebedee met his death caused his accuser who had come to gloat, though that gloating didn't last a full minute, to join the growing legion of Jesus' followers.

## Philip and Nathaniel

By the Jordan in February, 26 AD, Jesus embraced his cousin John. It was a clasp both strong and tender enough to last them both for the rest of John's earth-time. They parted, to not see each other again in this world. Earlier, Andrew and Simon had asked the Baptist, "Should we follow Jesus?"

John, their Master, and a brave man, said, "My work is finished. By and by, we are all to become his apostles."

Now Jesus with his first four followers, set out on the road to Capernaum. Trudging the dust, they saw Philip of Bethsaida coming along with Nathaniel, a friend. These two were also on their way to hear John. Philip, who casually knew Jesus, waved to them. They were friends, well met, and jabbering on eagerly in the early spring sun. Meanwhile, Nathaniel, less known to them, sat down in the shade. He was content to look on at a botanical patch, the flowers, the grass, there the brooch-like iris, a damson crocus, and the cyclamens, diaphanous. While the others chirped on among the slopes of early scarlet poppies, Jesus took James aside to outline the route they would take. In midst of gossiping and bragging, the tall Peter leaned down to the sparrow small Philip, "You know, we've all been waiting. He," dropping voice, Peter jerked his head toward Jesus, "he is the one. You should join us."

Philip, a bit of a bumpkin, clapped his hand to his mouth. What? Him? A nobody to be brought to share in a revelation? Quandary set in. What should Philip do?

"So," growled Andrew at the obvious, "go and *ask* him!"

## His Friends

"All right," said Philip. He went and asked. "Shall I join John, or my friends here who follow you?"

"Follow me," smiled Jesus.

Thrilled at the simplicity of it, Philip whacked his new Master on the back. Then stumped over to Nathaniel sprawled under the tree, leaned down, said, "Come on! Do the same."

"What him?" Nathaniel, no country yokel but a man of wit, cavilled. "Him, a carpenter? The 'Good out of Nazareth'? Hrumph!"

"Go and see!" Philip dared him, "Go on. Speak to him."

Challenged to it by the roadside, Nathaniel stood up. He was a handsome-souled man, avid for life. Under the few trees he walked back in their islets of shade, to have a look, to get the measure of the man. As he neared Jesus, Nathaniel stopped. He looked straight into his face. But it was Jesus, having seen Nathaniel sitting in the shade, who chose him. "There's no deceit in you. Some good doubt, yes! But," he smiled, "follow me!"

Hearing his voice, Nathaniel simply said yes. Considering that face, a life-longing in him came to rest. Feeling just a tiny touch light, like a man mildly sun-struck, Nathaniel stepped back. He walked to his friends, his face in a melt of wonder, and said, "But he *is* a Master."

For a man whom Jesus once described as "one without guile," Nathaniel could be a very funny man. Quite a jester, his was a jab of humor, but always with a twist of good reason in it. When the Master's absence was to slump them into depression, Nathaniel's wit perked them up. Hands leisurely folded behind his head, big snorts of laughter booming, Jesus would lean back, enjoying Nathaniel's perorations on matters both weighty and trite. Everybody was to like him. All except, that man of no irony, Judas Iscariot. Nathaniel, Judas had determined, was a clown. Once he even stormed to Jesus to tell—believing he was being revelatory when he was merely acting the spy—that he, Judas, was sure Nathaniel was but a clown.

"But Judas," from Jesus that undefended smile, "it's not the Father's will for you to be always serious. Let me say this to you: people ought to have fun! And more of it! So do what's yours to do, Judas. And let Nathaniel give an account of himself to God."

Judas took these words about "fun" as yet another put-down of himself.

Prone to be judgmental himself, Nathaniel had been stopped dead on that road when he tried to size Jesus up. The personality wave from him smote Nathaniel like the sun, personality being the subject that engaged Nathaniel the most.

"God *is* person, a personality," had been a thought he recurrently had—a subversive one for a Jewish man. Of course, Nathaniel knew, the Deity was not only personality, but what in God was personal was here, in this man. Facing Jesus on that road in Galilee, Nathaniel saw in him the personally supreme, the human aspect of the Creator. Personality, he had worked it out, was the face God turned to this part of the creation. But such thoughts as he had, Nathaniel knew were only glimpses of truth's full picture, just fade-ins-and-outs, not the full circle of its eternity-range. In the spring light he had met a human whose absolute reality of person plunged him to a level of reverie, lucid and calm. At first he resisted it, being restless by habit and reluctant to settle on any point. But then Nathaniel weighed it up, If that supreme event on the road was just me wanting God to be in that man, then perception is unreliable, and thought is not to be trusted, the world mad, and I am insane. Either the experience I've just had comes from reality, from God himself, or nothing does. In any case, the person of Jesus was worth the risk of his reality-sense. "Because, if this is not so, then after this," he decided, "nothing else matters. Though through him, everything does."

Of Nathaniel's faults, almost the only one was pride. Pride was that good thing of human self-respect, if not carried too far, but Nathaniel did, he carried pride too far. He judged others against himself. He would say, "I wouldn't have done this," or "I wouldn't react like that," But then, he could also see the boorishness of such personal assertiveness, saw what it was actually concealed hostility. The great knack Nathaniel had was the capacity to quickly reverse himself. So far, his best reversal had been on that spring road of Palestine poppies when he looked into the face of Jesus. Nathaniel was to love his Master's huge tolerance, a man so allowing and free, Jesus saw things for what they were, and like life itself, he let them be.

After all that was to happen to them, Nathaniel would be the most accurate in relaying the words Jesus actually said. He was a universalizing sort, never wanting a perception to be just his. If a truth wasn't other's reality also it couldn't at all be his. For him it was, "There is no truth alone." Never wanting to shine with a private vision of his own, the eccentric's glint of a "personal truth" gave him the shivers. Your truth had to be a part of others' truth. For it not to be so was to have found neither truth nor the love of others.

Nathaniel was to go first into Mesopotamia, then to the Far East whose peoples easily took to the message he correctly spread, the plain and happy tidings of Yeshua. He baptized those who would receive it and believed. There was a rumor that he was flayed alive. But Nathaniel died peacefully and very well received in far-away and congenial India.

Philip was a clod. But his foolishness wasn't vicious. He was short, gabby, a bungler, and an incompetent. But he became the steward of the twelve. The ordinary people who were to flock to Jesus were glad to see a Philip, a plodder like themselves, in a position of such usefulness. As a steward he did very well. Little things he could do in a big way. Jesus nicknamed Philip "The Curious" for continually asking questions. But his questions had no bite or discernment, were off the mark, sprang from a failure to grasp what was happening around him, and had no sense of timing. Philip was inadvertent, had no ear for what was going on, and would often barge in, or run on, ludicrously beside the point, elaborate or mistake the issue, silly and dull in a boring way. He would cut in on Jesus, the Master just on the brink of clinching a point, with some blather about the zizzing of a fly. Jesus made no eye-rolling faces of long-suffering at Philip's foolish prattle. Philip did not mean to subvert or annoy. He just did it. Interestingly, Jesus never reprimanded him. For after all, their Lord and friend was far more fascinated by human beings, even by Philip's non-sequitur gaffes, than in his own sermons.

Philip's was not, like that of the others, an act of visionary conversion, the "Abandon everything for the unknown" summons of Jesus to them. He was more of a meanderer on the path of the old dispensation. The received truth of the time was when the Kingdom arrived the Law would come to an end. With John the Baptist, Philip thought the age of Law was coming to an end. Though Jesus did not so much replace the Law as reveal its integral practice, Jesus *was* the kingdom for Philip.

Not very bright, and therefore very dogmatic, this apostle was fearless in death. His wife stood at the cross of Philip calling out to him to hold steady in faith. She was only silenced by the stone that sent her to her own death. Leah, their eldest daughter in whom an unexpected acuteness had gathered, became the prophetess in Hierapolis. A priestly and reverential woman of grave insight, Leah continued the work of their faith.

But right now with his first six envoys-to-be Jesus arrived in Nazareth. They were to rest that night at his boyhood home. The old white house was now lived in by his brother, Joseph. At one point in the jollifications, Jesus left. Slipping away, he took to every nook of their Nazareth house, searching for any scrap of writing ever written by his hand. Joseph his younger brother went after him. And found him, tearing pages of papyrus and scraps. Joseph stood by, half a barley loaf in hand, the others too, coming to watch as Jesus systematically tore up every parchment or board on which he had ever written a word.

So much for his attitude to the written.

Nor were the apostles ever to see him write again, except once in the transitory grains of dust. Cautioned by that, and to the loss of posterity, they would be tardy to record in writing their own experience with him.

He was setting out now to Capernaum. He was to go and see his mother. Before he went, Jesus sent his friends on to Cana where there was to be a large village wedding. Everybody in the district was invited.

Before the apostles left, they talked over with some of Jesus' family, the things they heard and saw at that baptism over by the Jordan. On hearing these recountings, young Joseph remarked, "Perhaps, Mother was, after all, right; maybe our strange brother *is* the king prophesied." To those who loved him, there was no question of it; of course their great brother Jesus was Israel's true king to come.

*Chapter XII*

# Waiting in Galilee

A few days ago, shelling peas in her Capernaum garden, Mary had been listening to her sons, Jude and James. The boys were describing to their mother what they witnessed at their brother's baptism.

"Ah!" cried Mary "I knew it! At last! He is to assume his reign!" Like that ardent, patriotic girl who had been greeted by an angel of the universe, then misconstrued it as a partisan triumph, Mary clapped her hands, "My son! The supernatural King of the Jews!"

Her sons looked uncertainly at their mother. Mary the unstoppable! Her ambition for her first-born knew no bounds. Her boys had their doubts about the exact nature of their brother's calling. What they had no doubt about was—it would be remarkable.

This time, the stay of Jesus in Capernaum was brief. But how glad were his local friends to see it—his expansive, lightsome manner was back. He had his former ease of touch and word. As in youth, his conversation was receptive and spirited as he joined in around the evening table. But the longings of the race had been re-gathering in Mary. She was hoping her son would at last manifest, what she always knew he must, that miraculous power with which to reclaim the nation's respect. She wished he would reach out and claim his destiny, David's throne. In this hope Mary had been dropping hints of her expectations to her neighbors. In fact, she was airing them to everyone. Palestine, warned Mary, was to be stunned by wonder-works from her son.

He, of course, knew nothing of it.

## His Real Life

The family of Jesus set out to walk to that wedding in the village of Cana. On the way, Jesus sidled up to Mary, to chat and bandy about with his mother again. They walked next to each other like that, shoulders bumping and snug, side by side. They spoke of the small home things, laughing a lot. Risking their cheer, he had to say it, just once more, and just in case, "You know, don't you, I *am* waiting. But only to do the Father's will."

His mother nodded. But knew better. To Mary's mind the vagueness by now had to be over. The time had come; Jesus was to seize the moment, assume his authority as Messiah. It would be in the grand style described by the prophet Daniel, an assertion of authority and grandeur. A Queen Mother on the way to her son's coronation was Mary all the way to Cana.

Once there, she behaved according to role. When they walked into the wedding reception, bouquets of wild flowers everywhere set, woven walls of grass and palms, the news of Jesus had already spread. Nearly every person from that thousand at the wedding was jostling to greet the famous Galilean. But he only stood about, awkward. Afternoon was passing. And still no miracle. So, clasping James by the hand, Mary came to him.

"When," they politely but insistently asked, "When will you manifest yourself as the Supernatural One?"

In a way that Mary and James recognized from other times, they saw his face flush. "If you love me," for the hundredth time he rebuked them for this, "wait with me on God!"

Mary lapsed. She withdrew. She grew fretful. Then depressed. And Jesus had left. He had gone outside. Among the early evening shades of olives he was trying to stop feeling hurt. Yet again, the old glory-hunger had blocked his family from hearing him. The wedding carousals and thrumming inside, he stood in the garden, willing the hurt to go. And when the shadows had shifted, and he was sure he understood them, and sure he did not hold it against them, he returned to join in dancing with the crowd. But from the ring of dancers, some woozy folk were wafting looks to him as abased and panderous as to a king. Jesus snapped shut. He drew his six friends outside, and warned them, in a voice peremptory, "Do not think I have come to show my hand this way!"

His friends listened, saying nothing, faces troubled.

But when the bridegroom's mother flittered over and whispered in a panic to the mother of Jesus that the wine was running out, Mary piped up with neighborly helpfulness, "Don't you worry, my dear. My son will fix it."

*Waiting in Galilee*

Over the years since Joseph's death, Mary had always relied on him. As if grooming him to assume command, she always turned to him at every crisis. Mary had further motives this time.

"My son," came Mary tenderly to him, her face at its most affective tilt, "they have no wine."

"What!" his stomach sinking, he hollowly asked, "what have I to do with that?"

"But," Mary looked her most beseeching, "I think your hour has come. Couldn't you help us?"

"Again I tell you, I have not come to do things in this way. Why are you always at me in this matter?"

"But my son," Mary broke down, "I promised you would."

"What," he tried to keep calm, "have I to do with such promises!"

Mary burst into tears. And Jesus, all judgment dissolved with pity for this hurt woman, was overcome. "Do not grieve so!" he stroked her dear face and locked her weeping form in his arms, "How often have I said," his voice broke, "I am not to work signs and wonders. And yet, I would gladly, if only God . . ." He stopped.

Turned around. Something was going on.

Shouts! People were hooting. Children running. Somebody squealed. Servants were dashing about. On shoulders were borne pitchers a-brim full of best wine. The guests were swinging around. Mouths agape in wonder at Mary's most miraculous son. Crammed into a corner, hemmed in by squawking squads, he was the last at that wedding to realize; what he wished in his heart had come to pass. The instant he could, he slipped out. And found a place he could be alone in the late evening garden.

He leaned against a tree. The "miracle," he was reasoning it, must have been with the Father's will. For without it, the change of water into wine could not have happened. This had to have been the process; he had desirously thought of a thing, and since it was not averse to God, it was. Now he was embarrassed. Even cross with himself. Why had he not watched for that time-factor in his wish, which, the celestial host at all times present to him had necessarily and immediately accomplished. And it had happened, but a "small miracle" of some little symbolic elegance for those of spiritual mind. So then, he thought, "All right. So be it." And reconciled himself to it.

But he went and fetched his friends, took them to the side to say it yet again; No, he was not the Messiah! They should await no such signs. "Look how they believe now!" he wanted to joke it away, but couldn't, "But it's only because of an unusual event. And that's not a loving of God. It's not what belief is!"

And then, though the deepest of thinkers, Andrew crushingly asked, "Are we then not to be counsellors in your Messianic kingdom?"

His grimace of rebuke at Andrew looked witheringly pained.

He drew apart. His face ashen, he stayed under the olives in the night. Alone through the lustreless dark, he sat awake and thinking. Far from the nuptial celebrations, under the gloom of Cana's sky not lit by any moon or star, he had to digest; his friends, chosen out of all the world to take the message, had understood almost nothing of the kingdom being a spiritual realm. In speaking of power, how often had he already said secular sovereignty does not matter. There was a kingdom of spirit so exceeding, so out-stripping of that. But their idea of Messiah was set. Their minds had been kindled by tradition, by miracle-workers, even with the Resistance Messiah of the Zealots, a restorer of territory and rights. But Jesus was not that. And, perhaps he did have to face it, his followers may never see him in any other light. He was beginning to glumly realize there might be no other public role from which to say what he had to.

Through his hours of desolation the earth slept on. All night he stood or sat, staring down on the ancient, pale soil of Cana. He stayed there until the sky began to blush. In the cheerless morning he returned for breakfast. Disappointing them yet again, he only spoke briefly of John. Quite terse, he said, it was befitting to wait until the Baptizer concluded his part of the work.

Later, and again dispiriting them, he only said, "Go back to your nets. Go, earn money. It is needful for you to provide enough for your families for the times you will be away from them." He, himself, went back to work at Zebedee's, saying he would see them in synagogue the following day.

On the third of March, 26 AD, at the Capernaum synagogue facing the sea, Jesus read from Isaiah. His mother, Jude, James, two of his sisters had come to listen to him. On this Sabbath as he turned to the congregation, all eyes were moist and tragic with pleading. He tried not to be dismayed. Their hunger for magic and miracles grieved him. But at the end of Scripture, devotedly, even mutedly read, in a half whisper, he said, "Only be patient. And you will see the glory of God."

The feeling for him at the synagogue contracted. He didn't seem to be delivering. The promised implied by his being had waned. Furthermore, that afternoon when he spoke to his friends by the shore, it was again only about waiting. Waiting! Though welcoming the many incidental people now gathering to him, to his own small band of brother men he austerely said, "Return to your work. Don't make noise about me. Remember, the kingdom is not to come with glamor, but in the great change the Father will have caused in your hearts. Be patient." he said it flatly again. And again, "Make yourselves ready for the call."

A few days later by the sea Jesus cautioned his listeners; this world would stumble at what he said. A sign-seeking generation would be slow to recognize in the plain word of a plain man, the revelation of the Father's love. Nor could the crowds on the sea's reedy shore hear his words exactly. Mystics and Essenes, Nazarites from Engedi, they stood with his apostles that time. Many from this throng saw him, perhaps unavoidably, only by their own lights. Some, it was true, did see the light of truth in him, as John had bidden them. But those not well disposed to the ordinary things he said, experienced only their own sensation of him, and hardly the personal force of a man anchored entirely in the transcendent.

Jesus only smiled, knowing this. By the water's edge he bowed to pray in that slow, fruitless and uncomprehended beginning with them. "Father," his voice was hardly more than a whisper, "I thank you for these little ones who, in spite of their doubt," he looked out to sea, "even now believe."

The waiting continued. That spring he met with the apostles more than a hundred times slowly preparing, unfolding their task: in a world of nationalistic fumings, of ranting politicals and rivalrous clans and castes, his almost inaudibly quiet message to be borne abroad and spread about was only the good news of God's love.

Then matters rushed to a head. A runner burst into the Zebedee boat shop where Jesus was working. "John! He's been arrested!"

It was a Tuesday, the eighteenth of June, 26 AD. Jesus laid down his carpenter's tools for the last time. "Let us make ready," he turned in the hour of his Father, "to proclaim the word." And arranged to speak at synagogue the next Sabbath.

This time when he entered, all kinds of people were present, farmers, politicals, land workers, agriculturalists, owners, merchants, even spies from Jerusalem. Jesus faced them. All faces looked up. They had come to judge his hour. And his hour was now.

"Truly, I say to you," like a bar of light, his voice cut the silence, "the Father's kingdom is here. It is here among you. You carry it in yourselves. But the kingdom is neither glory nor might. It is a realm of souls, of Jew and gentile, male and female, rich and poor. Nor does it attain to full fruit quickly. It's not a reign of power and plenty, nor meat and drink, but the service of God."

"Love," he was saying, his voice moving through the air, "Love everyone. For everyone has a soul. Which means," he let go the full volume of his voice, "you are to love your foes."

If, to the ear of the nation present, his word "Love" sounded like suicide, it was because suicide it was. By saying to them "Love everyone," he was making an end to the nation as themselves. By saying "Love," he was demolishing their obsession with enemies and self-defense, with fear and blame. Those who heard him at the synagogue reasoned, and correctly, "Didn't loving everyone else mean you weren't better than them? Which meant "Love" was the end of yourself! Unless, unless... A few there trembled on the brink of the new comprehension to which he was taking them.

And he was. He was taking them away from themselves, away from the nation, away from their story, away from its history, away from their own God-favored race, away from the family itself. He was turning people to a new identity, to be face to face with the Father, whose beloved child everyone was.

The people who sat at the synagogue that June were flabbergasted. Forlorn and oppressed, the Hebrews had wanted change. And they wanted it right now! But he was saying, change was as slow as the growing of a tree. They wanted an end to insult, an end to Rome's atrocity. And he was saying, wasn't he, Earth's rule didn't matter. They wanted the tyrants who tortured them smitten. And he was saying, "Turn your cheek." They wanted their enemies revenged and slain. And he said, "Love your enemies." They saw the Kingdom being for the righteous. But he said, "God also loves those who sin." They saw the Kingdom as the rule of their kind. And he said, "No! Heaven is for everybody."

Men of position and politics detested him for that. For what he said made a nonsense of them. He made a nonsense of their surge and assertion, a nonsense of their vehemence and charge. His own passion was for a thing as small as a seed. While their passion was superiority, to rule with it. But, said he, there was no rule like that. Or the only rule was, a matter then unheard of—Universal Love. Love was the thing, the one perfect thing, and he asked them to do that. "For," his voice hurled at them in a superflux of charity and ardor, "has the Father not said of his children, 'It is my will that they be perfect, even as I.'?"

When his congregation heard all this, most of them were so galled and furious they just couldn't believe it.

Yet, in about one third of those present, his words had begun a kind of rapture. They felt as if they were hearing the real destiny of their race, chosen indeed, to host the good news, and therefore be a people of universal significance. He had opened a dimension outside politics, beyond history, the past, beyond wealth and all circumstance. He was opening a new place in the soul, a liberty which everyone knew was there but hadn't the faith to live in it. To those who believed him, his words were felt to have sprung from the core of reality itself. At the radiant end of his words these few felt, God must be like him, if God was ever in a man.

Another third were methodically assessing what he said. These were those who saw the evils they continually suffered as coming from outside themselves. Illnesses were caused by demons. Their anxieties were caused by their enemies. Their chronic mishaps, fear, and terrors were caused by the evil greed and rubbish of outsiders.

And now here was this man offering to put them in touch with those others, to put them in touch with themselves, and in potential, was he not saying, with the universe itself! This man, he was a devil! At the very least he was a rascal, deeply offensive and scandalous. They mentally totalled what he had said, drew the line of self-preservation under it and then added it up. The sum of his message was suicide to identity, an insult to dignity, a demeaning of rights. What's more, you couldn't prove it or touch it, or buy and trade it. It was immaterial, and neither nature nor the world provided any proof of it. His was mischievous, dangerous news about the Kingdom of God.

The last one third at the synagogue neither accepted nor rejected what he said. They were certain, despite the man's composure, he was beside himself.

They thought him, quite simply, mad.

*Chapter XIII*

# A Man like This

"Find six more to take the word," two by two he sent them out, "so we can be a body of twelve in the world." A brisk embrace, and he let them go.

His first six fledglings set out. They were none too happy. On this, their first plod of a mission, they thought, "This isn't going to be easy. Doesn't even look very smart. And, is this *it*? The Kingdom's coming? An importunate scrounge for converts?" Not exactly what they had in mind . . .

How easy to sound off when in a group. But to speak of God, and to strangers . . . how intimidating was that! But as they made themselves do it, take the word, each apostle met with the people's raw hunger to hear. They found no need for much persuasion or palaver. Just the mention of a God who was your Father was enough to cheer people up.

While his fledglings were testing out surprising wings, Jesus visited his family. On walking in, he found his brother James insulted, Jude smarting, Joseph hurt, Simon in a snit. Now that their brother was beginning socially, how come they didn't get key positions? Why weren't they among the chosen?

"The chosen?" laughed Jesus, eyebrows flying up, shoulders apart, "My family in a public role? Wouldn't it be favoritism?"

But no. To his family it was a snub. And since Cana, the rift with Mary had widened again. Desolated by her great son's strangeness, by his content with being unnoticed and insignificant, she lived on, crestfallen in Capernaum, in an otherwise busy, decent house. Sometimes from the back yard, Mary might look out over their Galilee's pastoral scape, the stone fences, the

*A Man like This*

backs of sheep on hills, the few trees adrift in tides of land. Then she might lower her head and to herself admit that glorious career of her brilliant son was, if not yet a public fiasco, not going to happen. Humiliation, revival by hope, then dashed again by disappointment was Mary's experience in life, as might be that of anyone who aspired to exceed.

Meanwhile, and quite quickly, without fuss or too much choosy finicking about it, the six new apostles were found. They were accepted as brothers into their work, into a Brotherhood of no blood.

## Matthew Levi

He was a customs collector, and a publican. Contrary to prejudice about his occupation, Matthew was a man of depth. He had a welcome in him for things not yet known, even for those that went against the grain. In fact, the less he understood of Jesus, the more Matthew loved him. A good head for business, he got the nickname of "money-getter." It could have been disparaging, but it wasn't—more a sign of people's teasing affection. Matthew was wholehearted and a man of knack. Yet much of the time he felt a stranger in the world.

Matthew was not at all despised—only the feeblest of moralizers did that—no, he was admired for being financially stable, a smooth and pleasant social mixer. So, why did the successful Matthew feel rejected?

Matthew craved acceptance. Or he believed he did. He had early victimized himself by falling for the fallacy that whatever exists does so only if you can point to it. He feared that maybe humans were only their acts, the gain to be creamed off them. Such was the social clique to whom Matthew aspired—hard-nosed pragmatists, the demanders of results, the hell-bent notchers of the score. They were the ones to snort if you said life's value was the core of your personality, that you weren't what you had, but what you loved. They were the sort to go blank if told there was no merit in ruining yourself in any bolting, run-away ambition or wracking labor for things that made a loving life impossible.

But chained to his own self-estimate, Matthew looked with longing to those feted public figures—bankers, investors and merchants—wheeling and dealing and maybe grizzling, but in actuality, very married to the world. Matthew too wished to be thus espoused, to belong. He had always courted that world, always moony to it like a lover, seeing himself as abject to be outside it. He used to imagine that if he was looked-up-to, he would

## His Real Life

be a success. Success would give him the springboard to a stamina he imagined he had always lacked. So, feeling inferior and dejected, Matthew went on fantasizing, not a happy man.

Until he met Jesus.

One clear hour of listening to the man, and Matthew's hand trembled like a maid's to his neck. A worldly man with wife and family, when he heard the words of Jesus, Matthew felt the entire order of his values being annulled. He heard Jesus say the value of a life is the way you loved. His call was not to achieve, but to strive, the struggle to stay with your own vision, not its outcome. Success, Matthew heard, wasn't a "What" but a "How." It was the quality of your energy and courage, and so laughably obvious, it was not life that made your character, but character your life.

Hearing what Jesus said, Matthew felt it untie the knot of issues within him. On grasping the unforced goodness of the man, he nearly laughed with relief. On contact with the person of Jesus, Matthew saw his own truth, ghastly and radical; that no, he never actually wanted partnership with that tedious world's official measure of success. He thought he did; he had chafed and ached for it, envying every successful man for sleeping with that world. But from the hour he heard Jesus, Matthew knew the reason he had never been a success was that he had never wanted to get into that world's bed. It was he, *himself* who had come sideways to its portals, his wooer's nosegay tatty, holes in his shoes, his hair messy and unkempt. Thus had he ensured the world's rejection, knowing that a marriage to it would expose his real virginity, his soul's desire for the God, to whom alone Matthew could give his all.

So from when Matthew the publican got to know Jesus there were three odd things he began know: one, he, a father of four children, was spiritually a virgin; two, he was glad; three, he would remain so.

As to that contentious concept, The Kingdom, it was so fraught by the nationalist furore of Jewry's rulers, that Matthew was amazed to hear from Jesus this one single fact—to come to God, the one thing needed was as free and natural as faith. Of all of Jesus' miracles the greatest for Matthew was his own sudden comprehension of faith. That faith was not a feeling, or a conviction, or even an emotion. Faith was an attitude, a chosen position toward others, to life's knowns and unknowns. Faith was the faculty humans least exercised, maligned as passive and indulgent; but in fact, faith was an exertion; it was human thought's highest assertion. That, in a money-grubbing and matter-obsessed world, a man spoke of faith as the supreme act, struck Matthew Levi as a miracle.

Though warned off about writing, Matthew was to write screeds on the sayings of Jesus. Later, these tracts became the scribe Isador's "Gospel according to Matthew."

Matthew accepted funds for their work but only if freely given. He never asked for them. He gave almost all his money to their project. No one knew of his bequests, no one except Jesus. Matthew was morosely and mistakenly of the opinion that his dear disciple brothers looked down on him for being a government snipe, even a stool-pigeon for Caesar. How he would itch to tell them just whose funds kept them in bread! But he never did. He bit his tongue rather than boast.

He was penniless in the end. After his Master's death, Matthew went off alone, telling their story and teaching in Syria, Cappadocia, Galatia, Bithynia and Thrace until the irate Romans put him to death.

### Thomas Didymus

He was no quibbling doubter. Not a knee-jerk oppositionist, Thomas had an exact, loyal-to-the-truth type of mind. No carping critic or hair-splitter, he was a man with a precise sense of fact. Appointed Director of the Brotherhood's itinerary, he did best at executive work. He was accurate and not pernickety. Unfortunately, he was quarrelsome with a streak of suspiciousness. His personal clash would of course be with that splashing self-enjoyer, Peter, their giant-gestured leader. Cut down to size by Thomas in yet another swift riposte, Peter would bawl at him, "Mean! Ugly! Suspicious!" Indeed, how often was Thomas to clip Peter's wings on soaring bursts of oratorical flight! Yet Thomas was faultlessly honest, if a pessimist, since childhood.

He had a scientific slant of mind. But he turned its exacting analytic force mostly against himself. The tragedy of Thomas was his not being able to believe in the reality of his own experience. His incessant, badgering interrogation of it dissipated its contents. He had frequent, lucid presentiments made to his soul. He was the type to stop, consider and look them closely in the eye. He saw his own experience clearly, foursquare, intact. Then he destroyed them by intellectually questioning their basis. He had a withering doubt about everything. He was unable to see it wasn't about being brave, but a bloody-mindedness verging on madness to question everything. On the theoretical chance of a "What if?" he would dislodge any certainty he had. On the chance of a "But," or a "Couldn't it be?," Thomas could dismember any experience he had. Doubting the basis of every thought, he came close to driving himself mad. But he was not a man to do this from some pride of brain-performance, as did the cerebral bravos. He did so because he loved truth more than himself and his own sensations, especially if those made him feel lovely and cosy. If continually testing your perceptions is honorable scepticism, intruding doubt's corrosion into every affirmation could be suicidal irrationality. In the case of Thomas it was also some lack of faith that Reality's Actuator would not trick you so.

By the time Thomas came in contact with Jesus, he had almost lost all faith in the ability to know anything. In the incessant bouts of his mind's brawls with the validity of its own experience, Thomas was beginning to see a time when he was just too hurt and exhausted by uncertainty to stretch his hand out to God. He had begun to think, he might always be stuck in the whirlpool of his own doubts, when contact with Jesus let Thomas see something else, God's love. From that first meeting, one clear-eyed look, a quick embrace, and his transformation began. He grew more trusting of others. But he remained a victim of his own psychology, the accumulation of mood and melancholy.

Jesus was moved by the honest doubt in Thomas. It was a faculty in him Jesus admired with compassion. He felt for Thomas not to have discovered yet that the world of your mind was not who you were, that it too was transitory. You couldn't think your way through to reality with mind; thinking did not give you that. Mind being in the clutch of mechanical matter, its processes were inherently flecked with error and could not complete reality. What Jesus wished for Thomas was the faith possible to humans, who, caught in the yes/no, black/white split of mind and language, could not grasp the full framework of the universe.

The magnet for Thomas was the personality of Jesus. He loved the balance and symmetry of the man—the distribution of character in virile austerity and an almost mother-tenderness, firmness without obstinacy, helpful never meddlesome, calm but never indifferent, and without it ever being rude or rough, a deep, quiet strength.

Thomas always went for caution first. But he rallied quickly if he lost at debate. He held no grudges, no gripes. Like Philip, he wanted "to be shown," but on quite a different level. He was a man of unease, of very bad blue days, attacks of depressive, down-hearted doubt. Yet whatever happened to his emotions, Thomas never stopped being at the command of truth, an apostle. Intellectually, the man was a stalwart. Even at the nadir of disbelief in himself, he never disbelieved in reality, as he never doubted the existence of the constellations above his head. However *he* felt, the stars were still stars. They still existed. They shone whether he liked it or not. And basically, he did; he liked it a lot. And at times he received the grace to draw certainty from it.

The worst of doubt for Thomas was to be at the death of Jesus. But despite the destruction of all Thomas had come to love, God was still God, and still burnt his soul's one light. God was still intact in Thomas, even when he was not intact himself. Even when Thomas could hardly make any sense of himself, God did, God alone made sense, and maybe, in the end, even out of him, Thomas.

Of its own nature, it does what it must, and faith came back. But Thomas would have been helped far more had he not ostracized himself from others. After persecution had scattered his apostle brothers, Thomas went to Cyprus, Crete, and the North African coast.

He died in Malta at the hands of Rome.

### JAMES AND JUDAS ALPHEUS

The twins were fishermen, the simplest of men. Like most people of that region, the Alpheus boys were happy to be there by their small and delightful sea. Galileans tended to be mild and dreamy, almost visionary folk for whom the source of the world was naturally God. From of yore, Galileans saw the sky as heaven, saw angels in the empyrean, and, much like their ancestral Jacob who slept out under the stars, had visions of ladders to that sky. Lives lived in near perpetual contact with nature, Galilee's people often slept on hill slopes, on the shore, or under the trees sifting that strange, welkin-blue light of the stars. They would wake into the damson dawns of their hill-rolling region, cook a fish, eat some of that flat bread, work a little, not too much, dig the soil around the tomato and marrow, go and fish with friends a while—such was life. They lived outside a lot, in the air in which Jesus spoke, and nearly always under the sky, that sky being the essence of what he was saying to them—the frame and perspective of their lives.

The Alpheus twins were the steady workers and ushers when there were multitudes. They stocked supplies, ran errands, liked helping anyone. They were not mighty of wit or intellect, but, for the present, mediocre, and so, an inspiration to those of faint-heart. The crowds of those everyday people who teemed to hear Jesus took very well to being managed by the Alpheus twins, common chaps just like themselves.

Neither lowly nor pretentious, the Alpheus boys enjoyed living, liked just being themselves. Of Jesus, they couldn't at all grasp his mind, but felt the heart-bond between him and themselves. If the Alpheus two were not very bright, and even, what might reverently be called, "stupid," they had a real experience of Jesus in spirit. They believed, and experienced themselves, each to be God's child. And the same was true, they felt, of everyone.

These two men were the pure of heart he had spoken of at the time he was with them, and who, after he left, were to see him everywhere pure, but mostly in the setting of nature. When Judas and James Alpheus remembered the poplars beside the Hermon river from their journeys North with him, in their minds' eye they continued to see Jesus striding under them. Or, at day's end, gazing over the hills to the lake, they would see the land's dusky color and think of all the times he, their brother-friend looked out on all this too.

After it was over, and once home again and fishing in the sea, they saw him having fished here as well, and still fishing here in a sense, still smacking his lips with relish for the chives and the tomato-onion salad they were preparing, perhaps drinking some wine and laughing again with his intense capacity for happiness. They would recall his open face looking up, up to the stars at night, his eyes filling with the thought of Heaven's Father, then turn to them, with the same love.

With a simple heart-faith in Jesus, the Alpheus twins could never understand the work of the spiritual realm. They had only the vaguest inkling of the inter-galactic network of worlds strung into the ethical net of their Master's teachings. After his death, these two bucolics returned to their families and fishing nets, blessed by the four years spent with a godly man on earth.

## Simon Zealotes

Simon was a thunderclap. A rebel by temperament, he was by reflex on the side of protest. Saddled with the ego-urge to be different, he was naturally a Zealot. Though conspiring against Rome and bringing sacrifices of blood for your ideology was considered the height of social prestige, Simon was no vapid lackey toadying for the smile of society. He was a primitive. He obeyed his passions; he was rumbustious, a punchy, blustering man.

Detesting the detail, loathe to work out causes, he agitated himself into large and feverish generalizations. The most exciting one was patriotic zeal. He jingoed on about the Nation in flashy bursts. The Zealot-emotion stoked Simon like a fuel. The Zealots, thriving on a hissy self-martyring hatred, kept regurgitating atrocities, brandishing their garish holocausts with a program to attack anyone for it. As the Zealots' passion for their cause intensified, their ideals became hollow, smothering the individual, demanding rigid conformity to the collective demands of the race.

By the time he met Jesus, Simon had been losing impetus. So he had been redoubling his fanatical efforts. Meeting Jesus, a man in quest of no power, and Simon's face, that of the warrior-hero, melted into an almost unprecedented smile. Hearing from Jesus the ancient beatitudes of spirit, Simon's heart missed a beat, stopped, then struck up and danced. Here was a prophet not raving on about evil, or cudgelling the "sons of the devil." He was gentle; he cared for humans; he was vulnerable, undefended, a man of faith. For all his own proclivity to rant and declaim, the power of goodness had the strongest pull on Simon the Zealot. He never thought of himself as good; he couldn't have defined it, was himself unable to create it, but goodness was still the magnet for his breast thumping nationalism. When he met Jesus, Simon stood in rays before a man of great, effortless good, with no self-shine in him. In a world driven by inertia and dread, Jesus had that innocent, almost helpless power of all great people—a God-lit radiance joined to the nobility of a normal man who could be bruised and broken, broken to death, but not hurt.

Jesus was the most radical man Simon had ever met. Love was the most novel thing Simon had ever heard. Far from falling dead in him with a thud, Simon recognized love as the most revolutionary force, ever. When he heard of the Father-God's love for all the creatures, which, if embraced, would be Jewry's national end, the bolt holding together Simon's armory of locked-in convictions was turned. But not wrenched out. For had he let them go, his battened down and riveted opinions, then Simon's frantically constructed persona of national furore, of insult and offense would have fallen apart, and then his soul would have had to admit a universe of love. So, no, Simon's bolt did not fall out. But it was seriously loosened by Jesus.

He remained volatile, morose, patriotically fixated. In a genius-stroke for the appropriate, Jesus gave Simon the charge of the apostles' play-life. He became a person who, though unable to be corrected by what he beheld, could scrape the energy off disgruntlement and get on with the job. Simon was the apostle to be sent to any person stuck in the jaws of indecision. It took him at the most, a quarter of an hour to settle vacillation in anyone. He could cut through the walls of argument, and get to the crux of self-obfuscation and inertia.

In the company of Jesus, Simon was to go a long way towards opening himself to the terrifying instability of a larger vision of life. But his courage did not rise to the last act—Simon could never quite surrender the safety of thinking that his own people were a privileged and superior race, for the riskier grace of believing in the equality of all.

## Judas Iscariot

The man was serious, a seeker. Always feeling swindled as if robbed, himself having too little in fact, Judas was a vehement seeker. He was a searcher for everything outside himself. A seeker of such grabby insistence, his parents disowned Judas when he joined that outlandish Baptizer, the farouche John. And alas, the Pharisaic atmosphere of Jerusalem led Judas to value, not holiness, but righteousness. As far as his teaming with the other apostles went, he saw himself as a superior Judean among those low-breed, mixed-blood Galileans, a questionable bunch for Judas. In the eternal circus of the planet's warring latitudes, of rival North and South, of warring East and West, Judas and his Judean compatriots were much given to blackening the moral character of Galileans.

Well educated, he could think clearly about the objective. But somehow, never too clearly about himself.

When he met Jesus, Judas was charmed. His delight was in the Master's all-round person. When, at their meeting by the sunlit temple in Jerusalem, Jesus looked at him, no challenge in his eye, no confrontation, just a pure reception, Judas felt himself believing in the man. For the man Jesus, people had to pass no tests. He accepted you without proof of your lovability. He just looked at you, took you in, and accepted you, rogue or saint. Judas found in Jesus such a trustfulness as to be a basis for his existence. But this quality of Jesus also stung Judas with a fear as for lightning. A belief from the soul felt to Judas like it could take him over. Faith, the fulfilment of any other man, felt to Judas like a loosening of grip, losing all foothold in himself. Faith to him was like a destruction—his own.

Yet everything was going well. As treasurer, Judas was loyal to his office. Nor was he some cheap money-grubber, but impeccable about detail and intelligent. And the others, all sunny Galileans less severe than this prickly hedgehog of a Judean, couldn't help liking him. A stickler for organization, Judas showed tact in dealing with Jesus' financial style. And he needed it! In money issues the idealist's faith of Jesus was a trial for everyone. Yet Judas met the Master with skill and a measure of deferring trust. So matters for Judas were looking up. While Jesus looked on Judas with a friendship full of hope.

But Judas had some very loose, that is unexamined, ideas. One was about what others were supposed to have said. Or what they really meant. He often misinterpreted what was said by enemies and by friends. Way off beam, and at times he half-knew it, but he hung on; it was *his* position, he stuck to it. A man of puerile beliefs and suspicions to justify, he spent his life defending them. Not because they worked. Or even because he particularly liked them. He fought for his own notions because they were his. Feeling the resistance in Judas, no one ever criticized him. Never corrected, he felt an implied criticism all the time. Judas was sure he had the right to any emotion, so long as it was strongly felt. His feelings were always right, whether sore, berserk with jealousy, petty and miffed, they felt right to Judas, because they were his. If he hated a person, which he frequently did, well, that was all right; it's how he *felt*. That's how *he* felt! He had the right!

Jesus knew the sore spots in Judas. To him, Judas was an adventure in faith. Jesus hoped for Judas. He tried to help the man by always trusting him.

Though Judas had a fairly acute intellectual grasp of the truths Jesus said, somehow, love for the man did not follow from it.

On the teaching tours, Judas would listen deeply to Jesus, usually from the side of the crowd, or skulking down the back. When people first met Jesus their usual impression was of having been impacted by the maximum of human reality contactable here. This quality of his Master gave Judas pause. That pause opened into fields of bliss in which Judas could see himself no longer hurtling, shoulders hunched, head down, in a nightmare of incessant self-justification, but beginning to walk on level ground, a steady track to become an avenue of shine, and then walking on the air of faith, grateful and entire. Instead of receiving this experience of hope as a free gift to his heart, Judas, who never wanted to have something good in case it let him down, would ask, "What am I doing?"

## His Real Life

He had another weakness, that of "getting even." This came to a head when a woman, out of sheer adoration, broke a flask of oil at the foot of the Master, just to lavish it on him out of some private grief.

Judas could have spat! But strangling vocal expression, he squirmed instead, sickened by the squander of it. And the Master stopped him, and in front of other men, saying to Judas he should allow the love in others. To let others love. At that moment, a life-time's proud hurt organized into a wall of revenge. At this public rebuke all his hurt battened upon the one innocent person who stood at the crossroads of his life as it turned from a steady progress towards light into the chosen darkness of self-assertion. Judas would get even! He knew from then. Though in that second of imagined social humiliation, he did not yet know with whom, or when.

In time, his hurt came to see a timidity in Jesus. In his Master's refusing to assert the Jewish Kingdom, Judas saw a coward. Sure, Jesus was orating great things, but failed to use the power he had. This, to Judas, was a failure of nerve. He began to think of bringing his best friend to judgment—the powers of Judea would be so indebted to him for that—and, reasoned Judas, it might also be the best for Jesus. If Judas forced necessity, Jesus would have to act. Crisis would force Jesus to assert his real power. Why, he was helping Jesus to face who he was!

But there was a further step in this logic. It was to do with Judea's religion of no-life-after death. Jews had no views of the soul's growth after death, no on-going participation in universe reality. The Pharisees did have a "resurrection of the righteous," people who would live on in the flesh to be present to the triumph of themselves. Of course, such a resurrection was but a theory of revenge. But such was the complacency of their self-vindication. Now, reasoned Judas, if Jesus rose from the dead, God would be saying the best thing to humanity by that. Therefore the death of Jesus would reveal if Jesus really was from God, or a charlatan. Because, if Jesus did not rise from the dead, the future he promised humanity was a lie. And if death did not end in an eternal life in which we shall all share, then Jesus' crying out the love of God was a swindle meriting death. If Jesus did not rise as promised, he was just another immolated fool. And if there is no future for those who suffer, whether in evil or innocence, then there is no good on this earth, nor in the God that Jesus said was the loving Father of all.

Not a man to risk having faith in what his otherwise loved Master said, Jesus had to die for Judas to see if what he said was correct. No, Judas couldn't chance being wrong. He had to test it out. He wouldn't risk it, being a fool, either for money or for love.

Of course those pieces of silver meant nothing to one whose craving was for that far fatter red-herring of the world—to be the one who is right, and nobody's fool.

When it was all over, Judas had no more wish to live with himself. Lunging away from the palace of Caiaphas, the decrepit old wretch flinging the insult of silver at his ankles as he ran, Judas felt he was no longer really interested in the answer to his testing of Jesus. He didn't care if you lived forever, which you would if Jesus was God's Son. Judas found himself with no taste for eternity, no interest in reality and, how strange to realize as he ran, to have no fear of oblivion either.

As a last refusal of the realities of existence Judas took his own life.

*Chapter XIV*

# Waiting

Before the saying and sharing of the word, came the small, gray days of waiting.

Every one of his apostles was invited to live on the estate of the boat maker, Zebedee. Jesus said for them to do quiet work together, to learn and experience life, think about it, feel it right here in the region of the Galilee's sea. For soon, he said, they were to go on journey, taking the word to others.

But first, practicalities. Still not enough money saved for their families, and back to work they were sent. This meant the waiting was to stretch out for five more gruelling months.

And when they all went out fishing together and he rode with them the wavy expanse of that broad and running sea, often in boats built by his hands, how they loved to ride the bellicose waves; he, an expert with the sail, a sailor deft, and humorous man, all the while readying them for that more comprehensive public work for which they were waiting.

Also, in the Galil's glad land, Jesus set the day of Wednesday for their holy-day of rest. "Play, my children," he would open his arms as if to let go a bosom-full of larks. By this stage of his own needs, he took little rest himself. But for the pleasure of their company he often went with them.

The way he spent time with them, his friends wondered, "Was God like this?" They cooked and ate their meals together; they rowed; they mended nets; they hiked and drank. There was a lot of coming and going, much of frolic at their feasts together by the lake. There was something always festive and eternal about it. "Is this," they asked of one another, "how God cares for you, the way Jesus keeps company with us? Is he," they wondered, "telling us a story of God by how he lives?" They felt him being God's Word to them, just by the way he was.

These were months of learning. Of all the most surprising, he gave no precepts, no rules on how to be a righteous character. He gave good tidings instead; a new description of reality that let you contact your Father and learn who in reality you were.

"But first," he warned them, "Make no legends about me. My person is not to be your point. You are to do the one thing, the one thing only; speak of only the Father's love."

From the busyness on their faces, he saw, they, his brothers, would re-construct most of what he said. He looked up dismayed, looked out long over the hills, under the spring's light webbing of clouds. And knew this: his followers would join his message with their own concepts and make it serve other purposes, not his. Still, he went on trying.

"Now, take personality," his eyes passed back to them, "Consider it. The person you are is God's gift. Just as an infant is a personality-form of an ideal its parents had, so a child of my order, and I *am* a child," he touched his heart, "is a creative idea of the Father who gave my personality, just as he has given you yours. So, if God gives everything to everyone, who can have more, and who be given less?"

Personality is precious, he told them. Personality wasn't ego; it wasn't illusion, or a construct to dissolve in Nirvana, but God's most particular gift of growth to you. Spirit was personality's foundation. And you lived in perfect happiness if you let yourself be led by it. He told them, soul was what you had, Spirit was what is sent. If your soul turned to the spirit sent to your particular personality, then your soul knew, and your mind lived in the clear light of God.

"Where!" cried Thomas, "where is the *proof?*"

"Your own soul's eternal delight in its continuous sense of God's presence. You need no more proof than that."

"Why is this hidden . . . ?" grouched Judas, not happy to hear this but feeling excluded from the unimaginable generosity of it.

Jesus turned to him. "The Father doesn't hide." he said, "Humans hide from God in the mists of themselves. If you can't see God yet, Judas, have faith in your own spirit. Just go on and have the trust that one day your spirit will evolve in you a capacity to know God."

Some there thought about this. He said, didn't he, that his personality was the acting nature of God. If so, then so was everyone's personality that. He said each personality was an ideal in the mind of God. And, yes, his person gave body to this idea. His flesh spoke the word of God. And, wasn't it strange, but he even looked like what he said, a man who behaved how God might have, had God come into this time-space place.

As a Father-revealer, Jesus never pointed to himself, but always away. And now, instead of going on about who he was to God, he took the greatest leap of all, and told them who they were to the universe.

"This," with the derring-do of the risk-taker's smile, he opened his arms, "this is what's going on. The mind of God for you is Paradise. A universal circuit of spirit gravity is drawing everyone to it. It is the desire of the Father for you to be perfect citizens of our universe, yours and his. And you can do this." he said, "because this is the set-up. It is what's happening. And this world," he tried to hand-shape it, "is the arena for it. This sector in space-time is your training ground. Or, if you like," he swept with affection towards his fledglings, "your nest."

"But why?" asked Thomas, "Why all the struggle if this is the plan? Why aren't humans simply made perfect?"

"Because for the present, we are in a universe of ascent. You are required to evolve. That is, to grow, climb, and change. And no," he revealed to them another piece of upward nuancing that was radical, "you are not the "made-perfects." And, yes, there are such beings, the perfect are those who descend in the Creation. Their task is ministry and service. You are ascenders for now. After you attain ascent to your own perfection, universe roles are reversed. In the next universe age, all perfected humans shall be in service to those who are not. This is how the universe works. This is the universe economy. This is the process of the cosmos. Your endless being in it is the plot."

"But the pain!" screamed Judas.

"What is inexplicable here," the voice of Jesus bent delicately inward, "the scourges, the illnesses, the eviscerating cry of a child, or of a dog, all these Judas, will redound to the good in God. They shall be woven into a pattern of high value by the God-force evolving the universes."

Judas looked on, parched. Possessed of a hungry, of a famished, soul, how he craved to believe what Jesus just said! But faith as a soul-act sounded weak to Judas. He thought faith was static, a feminized idea; he was repelled by it. It seemed too small an act, but a sinew of the soul requiring

*Waiting*

attention and care. He didn't see faith as the soul's most muscled product, the choice to love. Or, he didn't see what would make you want to choose it. Yet, so drawn to him, Judas did want to believe Jesus! But preferring his own pride of proof, his own sense of self in the assertion of *"No"* to faith, Judas wouldn't take a leap and make himself have faith—faith could trip you up, and prove you an idiot. Though when he spoke, the words of Jesus unleashed in Judas torrents of love, he did not honor what he loved. Love made Judas feel weak and foolish in his intellect, just because he wanted so much for it to be true!

In their months by the sea, Jesus gave much by word, but far more by how he was. His behavior was the most radical with people who were socially held to be of less significance, like servants, children, outcasts, dogs, women. In the midst of his own teachings, should a child chance their way, he would stop to gad about with that child. Or, say, he saw an old woman wrestling with a load of wood, he would cut into his own speaking, and run across the road to greet her. He would stop with her, say his thrush-happy things, cheer her along, and then, listen intently to everything the old crone might gab. To their drop-jawed disbelief, they heard him declare; "Women are the absolute spiritual equals of men." The flat way he said this, it was an indisputable contention. He expected no remark on the obvious. When his men heard him say this about women, they gaped, not contesting it, that being an idea so outlandish that no male of that world had debated, let alone seriously let it into his head.

The religious leaders of the land had declared, "Forgiveness is by penance and sacrifice." The rabbis taught that the ignorant could not be pious. But they, his rowdy and raucous apostles were pious in their happy lives by the sea, if of rabbinic preaching, cheerfully untaught.

Still, the wait was a trial to their kind of men. They all wanted to perform. They hankered to achieve, to prove, to flame-out, each to be a meteor, a star. So one day, a bleak one for Jesus, itching for the deeds of pomp and power, Peter rounded on him.

"Say when, Master?" Peter positioned himself in front of the rock on which Jesus sat, bent over, fixing a net, "Won't you tell us? When will you proclaim your Kingdom? And won't you tell us the positions in the kingdom each one of us is to occupy?"

Jesus darkened. He unbent. He reared in fact from where he sat. He had no anger, but he had wrath, the terrific, dark, silent quality of it. His face raw with it, he beckoned to the others. "How long will I bear with you!"

## His Real Life

he roared at them, "Have I not made the kingdom plain! How many times have I said, mine is not a political kingdom. It is not David's throne! How could it be you still don't understand? The kingdom is God's coming to the heart! So hear me again! Hear me this time!"

His friends were at a loss. The kingdom he spoke of, the personal, unproven quality of it, caused their drive for dominion to ebb. They stood about, stalled, scratching noses, pulling at ear lobes. After a nippy little while of this, Thomas with his flair for the transcendent, said, "To this coming kingdom, whatever it is, even if I don't understand it—I give my loyalty!"

So they stayed with him. They stayed because he didn't speak like a prophet or a rabbi or an oracle. Truth came from him as from one in whom all authority dwelt. And though he roared at them, "Find God in your own experience! Not in miracles!" for all his ferocity at these times they were coming to know him as a friend, their best friend in the world. And you could never desert a friend. They loved him for the feeling he had for everyone, for every woman and child. He felt what others were, felt what lived in every person.

This could have easily meant that his human heart would be continually breaking. For it was not the case that knowing more, Jesus suffered less. It was the reverse; his love being limitless, he suffered more for human refusal in the face of so much good. Because he loved more, he suffered more. After all, by loving less, you suffer less.

But his heart was also much regaled and made very happy by them. Jesus loved them, his larks, his lambs, his friends and fledglings, now preparing to fly. It is true that in these months he could have taught them far more effectively. Had he invoked the unlimited power that was his, the speed of his teaching would have been stunning; he could have had instant effect. But he was content with how they were naturally, their fumbling natures, their blanks and stumbles, their hum-drum ordinariness for which in the power-scheme they may have been insignificant. But he liked it like that. He liked the least dramatic, liked the slow, liked the natural pace. A tender man, he avoided all show of power as he went about the vastest job of a universe with them.

As for his own family, these months of public inactivity were the worst. Each brother, sister, and even his mother, everyone, except Ruth, had withdrawn from him. His heart they loved, but they were stumped by the nothing to show for it. If they ever came to visit, it was only for brief, eye-darting, must-go little chats. If they ever said anything, it was only to say he should come home, where he belonged, to home with his own, with them. If he wasn't theirs, Jesus seemed not to exist. When they met him in the region by accident, they would stay a minute, smiling inanely past his cheek, or even rolling eyes of censure behind his back. In a huddle among themselves, they bewailed that he had offended the local mores. Indeed, he had scandalized those of the pious who did not want God to be for criminals, drunks and whores. His family gave up defending him from the respectable clods of the neighborhood. They hung their heads, unable to weld their brother's doings to the grid of their own thought. At times they even scowled at him, hurt.

His family came close to seriously believing that he, once the epitome of their family's sanity and sense, was mentally disturbed.

*Chapter XV*

# The Ordination of the Twelve

His twelve were waiting, tense. Their excitement grew. Any day now, they were to be called. Yet, the more they knew him, the less of him could they encompass, the man he was. He was grand; he was aloof; he was a lamb, as meek; he was a lion, as stern, as uproarious as that. Apart from spite and contradiction, everything was in the man. Was that independence of his, his toughness? He seemed to want nothing. He relied on nobody. As for the power of liberty in him, how they wanted that! It charged people to him like pins to a magnet. And the man never forced a thing, he didn't even try; he never pushed; he premeditated nothing. He meant no effect. He just purled along, a river in its bed, flowing deep in a trust that never failed him. About to begin wider public life, he still seemed to need nothing—no one's agreement or good opinion, not even his life's safety, far less its meaning from anyone.

From the time he breasted Capernaum's hills, the people of that region took one look at him, and followed. When he talked people listened. One word, and they were his. He opened his mouth, and God came out of it. His words were a miracle of the soul, of soul turned inside out. A man of gentle presence, when people heard him, strife and ambition went quiet in them. They looked at his face and felt ferocity quench. With him, people became themselves. When he described their place in the universe, the obsessed became free, the melancholy glad, and the weak strong. On looking at him, people thought, "He looks like God, if there is a way God could look."

## The Ordination of the Twelve

The man called on no magic. All came from himself. He gave no doctrine, no techniques or initiations, no gnosis or mystic formulas. He asked the one thing—that people believe and love. He had nothing to say about norms, far less of special states. A barefoot man, he walked a ground shared by everyone. But when he looked you in the eye, you wanted to get your own life right, to clean it up, to set it free, to find your truth. That's how he was.

No longer fledglings and nearly groomed for the flight, the apostles hung about their creaky boats. They tinkered with the tackle and nets, kept in close, one eye on Bethsaida's shore.

One day in January just before midday and one of the twelve looked up. A way down the beach they recognized his stride, strong and easy along the shore. His arm rose. He waved. From that sea-life he was calling them. He was waving to them, "Come! Come!" They came running on the sand, sprinting in fact, and when they were all in the one place together they struck out as a company to the high lands of Capernaum. For once they were silent, they, his more or less garrulous men. During these months of inaction a personal sharpening had taken place in each, a pointing of themselves, an offering up.

When they were seated about him in the thicker grass of Palestine's winter, he opened his arms. "My children," when he used this expression of Semitic affection, that smile, a beam of blue-green iridescence, came from his eyes, "My children, the hour has come. Today you become messengers of the spirit. You are to carry a light that will serve the earth. It is true," he entered his theme, "sheer faith will let you into the kingdom. But saying 'Lord, Lord' is not enough. Show your heart by what you do. For it will not be by your words, but by the lives you lead, that people know what you love."

He stood up. On the hill the silence was such that every man around him knelt. He went to each one in the circle. He began with Judas. He placed his hand on each man's head, blessed each, praying in quiet as he did. Afterwards, every man embraced Jesus, not one saying a word.

"And now, my loved ones," his voice rang in the greeting of a new start, "you are citizens of a heavenly country. So," he leaned forward, one elbow on his knee, "keep what I am about to say. For I send you to bring freedom to the souls of captives, joy to the fearful, and healing to the sick by the will of Heaven. Now, say this to the distressed:" As he began, his listeners in the winter field heard the human sorrows turn into beatitudes.

"Happy," he said, "are the poor in spirit, for theirs is the kingdom of heaven.
Happy are those who hunger for righteousness for they shall be filled.
Happy are the meek for they shall inherit the earth.
Happy are the pure of heart, for they shall see God.
Happy are they who mourn for they shall be comforted.
Happy are the merciful, for they shall obtain mercy.
Happy are the peacemakers, for they shall be called the sons of God.
Happy are they who are persecuted for righteousness sake, for theirs is the kingdom of heaven."

For a while they remained. Silent there, they sat. No words to be said, each one sat in a beatitude as if inside a green wave of love. He sat turned towards them but unmoving under the sky. Birds winged by. The flat light shifted, turned gold.

They began to talk. The poor, he was saying, they are the seekers, those who feel unsure. So, they were the ones still able to receive, able to be taught.

Of true righteousness, he said, "It is not a 'Thou-shalt-not' but the love that goes out and does." Of meekness, he said, it wasn't fear, but the spirit of waiting in a person, faith in the friendliness of the universe. Of purity, he did not only mean purity in sex, but more that pure and unmixed faith people ought to have in one another. Of mourning, he said, it was to be tender, not to hide the heart. And mercy, it was the essence of the outgoing of kindness. As for peace, it saved a person; peace healed greed and race antagonism. And children, they all agreed, were the natural relievers of suffering, the peacemakers. You could see it by how they liked playing together.

After these words on the green hill, he sat looking out on the Galilee's terrain absorbing the winter shine. Time passed in the sky, over the hills, the sea. They heard an odd cricket whir. The grass tick. And when a little later the sky turned the shade of stocks Jesus went down the thin path from the hill, and walked alone on the strand in Capernaum.

Later that night, in Zebedee's garden, he said, "Be re-born. Be like little children. The old righteousness was by good works and fasts to secure the Father's favor. But let your new word to the world be Truth, Mercy, Love."

The teaching had begun.

## The Ordination of the Twelve

Asked about divorce, he only said, "Learn the laws of human relating for yourselves. Though, of divorce, I will say, while Moses looked with favor on such things, it was not so in the days of Eden."

"Of reality's many aspects," he said, "always remember, there are two view points, the one of humanity, and the one of eternity."

The warning about self-centeredness, "Do not expect others to live as you do in every particular. And keep in mind—I have sheep not of this flock. I am beholden to them also."

About courts of law; "Seriously, I tell you; do not strive with men. Return good for evil. And that mean adage of 'measure for measure,' don't make it your rule. Do your good deeds in quiet. And when you pray, go apart. Don't mortify yourselves to be seen by others. And, you know this already, as the lamp of the body is the eye, so the eyes you see with shall produce what you see. If the eye is generous your view shall be filled with light. And, my friends do not be concerned for your lives, what you shall eat or drink. Willing hands shall not go hungry, so don't fret for tomorrow; today's trouble," he shrugged with a smile that really knew it, "is enough."

Afterwards, each one there wanted to open his soul, to speak alone with him. So, starting with Peter, right through till dawn he took each one into the house and heard them out. He listened the whole night, saying much to each man. By dawn each of them had had the conversation with him that he craved. All except, snoring by the fire, heads flung back and mouths a-flap, the twins Alpheus.

"Shall we wake them?" Peter asked Jesus in the smoky morning, all their souls now sated and fed.

"No," he flapped his hand with a tired smile as he stretched, "leave them. They do well."

After ordaining the apostles Jesus spent another week with them by the sea. They still weren't sure. How would they speak? And to all the world?

"The world is not the enemy," he said. "Life is opposed to neither woman nor man. The condition of life is a divine neutrality that works along with you. And," he changed tone, "I say this for your work's sake; make no wars on injustice. But don't tolerate wrong-doing either." But he took no side in controversial issues, only stood back sympathetically, aware he was disappointing many of the sincere women and men, who, wanting to know what was wrong and right, were gathering in droves to him. Another thing, quite unexpected, he cautioned his heralds, "Don't just be on about religion. Since God has placed you into this world, this is the arena where you are to live!" Of humility, he said the snivelling sort was pure theater, and grovelling was ridiculous. True humility was the exact reverse, a superb kind of self-respect. Humility was right before God. But to keep your integrity was a duty.

"Courage" they heard, "is the heart of everything. 'Fear not' is our watchword. And, 'Be glad' is another."

"And value the whole of life," his voice gained volume in the evening's half light, "yes, embrace the lot, not just the virtue in a human. For, have I chosen effete carpers and moralizers, or twelve rugged forth-faring men?"

They set out walking with him. As he spoke, they noted what felt like startling new facts: there was no self-analysis in what he taught, no religious introspection. He encouraged no misty communings with the ether, no cerebral fretting for yourself, but vigorously said, "Be turned outward. Work on the level of daylight consciousness. Be informed, learned, tolerant. You are to have the one aim—to create in humans a new capacity for receiving truth."

Then he repeated it! That everyone was Heaven's dear and unreplaceable child. But some who were there couldn't grasp the depth and intimacy he meant. That being aware of who you are to God linked your seeing all living things as part of yourself. At the time, most people huddled under the shibboleth of the nation, a principle that said, life is a war of survival in which some of the living are your brethren, and some are definitely not. Didn't the Scripture stories of Cain and Abel, Jacob and Esau, of Isaac and Ishmael all prove that brotherhood is impossible? What Jesus said was an assault on the received view of "them" and "us," on separateness. He was saying, in the reign of God your worst enemy was God's equally loved child. That you would have to see the face of your enemy before you saw the face of God. Nor would you even know who you are to the Creator until every hand was joined. Although your soul was safe, indeed forever in God, until you joined hands with the world, you yourself won't know it.

And, they did not. Or mostly not. And yet, even without full comprehension, they knew the things now being said would change the idea of Man, of human identity, the velocity of history; these words would change forever the way people thought about one another and themselves.

On an evening of rain in the lamp-lit house of Zebedee where shelter had been given, they were listening again to him.

## The Ordination of the Twelve

This time he spoke of what they must be, not what they must do. Reared on a religion of strenuous ritual acts for salvation, they were bewildered to hear, "Your being must precede the doing."

The Hebrew religion was Law. Hundreds of obligatory acts. And an expectation of reward from God if you did this and that. But Jesus was saying something totally new—that if you *love*, just do that, then all the do's and don'ts would follow. Love would show you the sin; but no amount of fist-clenched threatening about sin would ever show you the love.

Not that he attacked the Law. He took the Law as a given. He took the Scripture to its spirit, took it past prudence, to the limit, and beyond. He said, "Love your enemies. Turn your other cheek. Give, not only your coat, but also your cloak. Be perfect!" No sage of Israel had ever laid down an injunction like that! He put fervour into ethics, put poetry into principles, added love to truth. And though the content of what he commended was the Law, he added to it the passion of charity, and not mere decency, but vivacity to morality, tenderness to goodness.

And then the waiting was over. Their going to Jerusalem was set. Before departure, John Zebedee asked Jesus the question that continued to trip them all up, "But Lord, what *is* the kingdom of heaven?"

On that occasion, daring a step further, he replied, "Heaven is not just doing God's will; it is having faith that the supreme desire for it will work."

"Galilee of the Nations" had in it all the flocks of the human stock. To Jesus, a Galilean, it was natural—strangers, sweet folk, scoundrels, degenerates—they were all real to him and one with him, and he dealt with them like that, whereas Judeans were prone to pounce with a sharp clout on the nose of anyone outside their own flock. For the most part, the land of Galilee was a lyrical region of nature, of summer trees, color and shades, of starry dreams, and hills, and ardent faith. While Jerusalem, the stronghold of Judaism, was a fortress, enclosing a huffy, screechy and odious society, baffling to most Galileans. In Jerusalem the proud *rigor mortis* of Hebraic monotheism did not permit the slightest detour outside their own fixed-in-stone idea of God, a paralysis of spirit suiting those of frantic and fanatical mind. Jerusalem was rigid, obstinate, no nature in it, or the nature there was unslaked and parched. Galilee was a dream, an idyll about God. Jerusalem was maniacal. True to Jesus' temperament, Galilee was his own. But his enthusiasm knowing no bounds, he had to take Judea on.

So they were going. They were taking leave of Bethsaida, leaving their raw, happy life by the sea. By the end of January, 27 AD, to the warmer zones of Galilee, the smallest shoots and buds had come. The kinfolk of his apostles and disciples were arriving to bid them farewell. Through the length of the day there was a merry ado of embracing, a flurry of well-wishing by the families of the men. Many hundreds of believers were going along with them. Many who'd heard Jesus speak, now wanted to go wherever he went. He set people's spirits into a wanderlust, their minds on voyage, hearts into quest. They were all to go on a sort of sacred travel, an excursion into soul. If walls are about partition, and fences about exclusion, then a life on the road with him would not be an aimless trek, but an exodus into the boundaryless. He was to walk the land and speak of God, including in his festive journey anyone who wanted to join, taking their thought to its essence, their knowledge to its roots, their feet into a life peregrine.

By the Zebedee workshop flowed a warm scene of arm-grasps and hugs. Amidst the goodbyes of departure, the apostle Andrew looked around. Jesus, the hub of the occasion, was not to be found. So Andrew went looking for him. He combed Capernaum for hours. From the round hills above he wound down to the shore, and there, in the distant sightlines of the sea, he saw him, Jesus, sitting in a boat. His broad back at an odd tilt, slightly bent. Andrew began trudging on the sand to him, his sandals abstractly slap-slapping. He mused as he went. What a master was he, drawing all these people back there, the youths and women of the district ready to follow him. Was it, wondered Andrew, because Jesus exuded the adventure-lure of a man relying not on walls or fences to feel at home within himself? He appealed as much to spiritual, fine-minded women and to scholars and red-blooded soldiers, as to uncouth fisher yokels like themselves. Women especially found in him the delicacy and acuteness lacking in their busy, custom-blunted men. Never flirting or preachy with females, his mind united with theirs easily and naturally, and with spontaneous effect, which was why so many women followed him, hearts kindled with enthusiasm, in a lyrical sort of devotion.

Nearing the boat now, Andrew saw his back was stooped more than a little. He stopped, startled. They, his apostles, had seen him in sorrow. But not this. When Andrew bent to touch his shoulder, he saw Jesus was weeping.

"Why?" Andrew asked.

Jesus turned to him a face torn.

## The Ordination of the Twelve

But he rose, got up quickly, just like that, out of the boat and stepped lightly to Andrew and, arms around shoulders, they were already strolling back. "Don't look like that," he was saying, "none of you grieve me. I am sad because not one of my family has come to bid us Godspeed."

Then Andrew realized: except for Ruth, his family had probably always misunderstood him. An expressive, self-involved clan, full of forthright feelings, they let their emotion of being hurt by not understanding Jesus keep them away.

By evening their hundreds had made it to Tarichea at the south west of the lake. Next night they camped near Pella. For two weeks they stayed, then travelled, a veritable exodus. Hundreds more were joining them. People came, drawn by lusty wanderers' tales, Greeks from the Decapolis, all sorts from Judea and Galilee, gentiles from Syria and Phoenicia.

Droves were flocking to him. Crowds sat listening. But, what was it really, as his disciples were worrying, what was the charisma of the man? Yet he never practised charisma. He abjured all program. He aimed for no effect. Nothing to gain, he would walk up to any person at all, deal directly with what was being said, never flinch, or get rid of a problem, re-cast or shirk a question. He never argued, just kept on going, seldom stopping to correct mistakes. No, not quite, because he did stop, yes, but only about God the one fixed-point in him. Otherwise, they never saw him flummoxed or vexed. He never apologized to anyone, for he meant all he did and did all he meant. Never distraught, at times he was sad. His expression, they saw, could steep into a sorrow as deep as the night. But most amazing of all, the man was faultless. They couldn't fault him. And he seemed to imply, faultlessness was possible for anyone. After several millennia of pessimist-based social control of humans brought up on the opposite, on the sin in Man, the potential of an achievable human perfection was heard as scandalous. True, his words did not always meet with understanding. But their echo lingered in the heart. And when people heard him, they felt his words press the chords of a new age, a time of universals coming.

One night in Amathus, he took his messengers aside. He wanted to share with them a tremendous truth. Not many were to comprehend it. And the organizations of the religions to follow would not speak of it. But that night Jesus wanted his apostles to see the wider cosmic mechanism in which the universes lived.

First, he drew for them the stupendous image of Creation. He spoke of the grand and awful times when the Father and his Eternal Other, the

Eternal Son, moved into space. "Understand," he said to them, "Love creates. Love *has* to create to be love. God creates because God is God. It is because the function of love is to extend, God's spirit fills all of organized space and holds every world. But God acts as a Father to human consciousness. He comes to humans by issuing into personality through the Creator Sons. I am," he touched the air, "such a Son sent to you, so that in me you may see who you are. As for me, I have come to learn what it is to be a creature, a human, a man. Which means if the divine becomes human, then the human becomes divine. This is my purpose. And this is your task. For you to know this is why I have come."

"And, my children, all of you are God's," he said. "When you really feel this," he made a gesture of inclusion, "you are hearing the law of the Universe. When God's will is your law, you are noble, but still a slave; but when his will is your will, it is because God is your life. Then you are no longer subject, but free. For then you shall see what you really are, and what you have always been."

Though not everyone there understood, this much was obvious; when Jesus spoke of God, he was telling people who they were. That God was your Father was your prime truth. This was the relationship that correctly aligned all the others. The knowledge of it set your identity into place. Accepting God as the source of your reality put you into the correct position towards it. From this it followed that the Kingdom could never be the exclusive place for a special person, sect, or race, but the experience of God by any individual.

"This" he stressed, "is all there is to religion. I am made flesh that you may know who you are." It was this simple. It was this good, this grand. But those with a grudge against magnificence refused it, just because it was magnificent.

Jews had long known God as the Father of their nation. And many were to know God as a Father of every individual. So the goodness was to spread from the nation, to the person, and out to all the planet's peoples, and to beyond the era. This was his message to them.

A vital matter, and related to all, he tried to replace in Amathus, was the offering of animal sacrifice. "Sacrifice your own pride, not animals!" he cried, "This is the true conquest! Their death purchases nothing. And God is not a merchant! You can't buy him with blood."

## The Ordination of the Twelve

Hearing this chime in with a recent thought he had, Andrew, sitting on the ground among the listeners, felt the millennia-old sacrificial system of blood-for-sin collapse into a heap of gibberish, no longer a part of him.

And then, about healing.

That world regarded illness as a sign of having offended God. But Jesus said illness was not necessarily because of a person's error. More often, it was a result of the unexamined laws of causation which humans would do well to comprehend. Humanity, he said, was placed into a universe of law, of dependable cause and effect. Not bothering to make the effort to know how it worked, made people slid lazily into magic, witches, denial, sacrifice, divination—all a nonsense of the imagination. The point was the behavior of matter had not been addressed. This was the issue people ought to pay mind. It was as obvious, down-to-earth, as unglamorous as that. When humans had the humility to learn their objective context and organized it properly, there would be a dramatic reduction in illness and suffering.

But the magicians and mystics who had been following Jesus felt fobbed off and soured by what he said. With dispositions to generalize and etherealize, they shirked the mundane and the specific. Of no mind to observe any detailed workings, they denied that there was such a thing. They did not care to investigate according to cause and effect, but only for the sensation of their own response. Dreaming of celestial favors and magical intrusions into reality for the correction of ills, when Jesus came on the scene they hoped he might explode reality, just burst it, and make a supernatural end to malaise. Since Lucretius a hundred years earlier, the miracles of the arbitrary gods had been held in derision by those lovers of the objective, the science-minded Greeks; but the Semitic mind's yen for the dramatic and marvellous didn't care for the carefulness of universal thinking. So when they heard the practical "how to" message of Jesus about dreary old cause and effect, they felt let down.

Nevertheless, the daily care and physical healing of the sick would be a part of the apostles' work from then.

One night on this journeying, James Zebedee, with his usual authoritarian fervor asked, "Master, how shall we learn to see alike so that we may have more harmony among ourselves?"

"Why exactly," Jesus was startled, "should you all see alike?" He got up from the stone on which he sat. He strode about in large steps, "Why would God desire harmony at the expense of your personality? Why would God want your originality sacrificed! When *that* is his gift to you! You don't have to see, or think, alike to have spiritual unity. Unity comes only from this, that you all have God's spirit."

Unity of spirit-purpose was all, he said. Unity of belief didn't matter. In the greatest diversity of thought there could still be unity of soul. You could best serve God as the individual he has made you to be. "So, act," he said, "according to the gifts he gave you of soul, and of body and of mind. It is not God's will that you be alike. And I warn you," he turned to them, rigorous, "never formulate mandatory beliefs as a way of controlling others who believe in God."

During the month of February the apostles taught in Perea at the ford of the Jordan near Bethany. Here they asked him did he deliberately ignore earth's great ones, the fortunate, the rich and the famed of the world?

No, he replied, of course not. They were equally loved. But the poor had been neglected by all the forces of history. So for now, they were the first with him.

Later, lighter of mood, he said that he saw himself more of a teacher than a preacher. "For example, look at Peter!" frisking the large, loud man, Jesus laughed with admiring pleasure, "He is a much better preacher!"

It was so. Peter was a man of grand, oratorical emotions. He would give big, stirring speeches to multitudes. It would be Peter's generosity to believe that experience of a life-turning kind ought to be shared, shown, heralded abroad. And it would be Peter's error to deem his own experience as a revelation of eternal fact. He had all the qualities of heart but lacked the restraint of accuracy, the necessary humility. Jesus was milder, slower to conclude, less dramatic. He spoke not to the emotions, but less sensually, through the mind.

Once asked why he seemed so unbothered by sin, he only said, "My purpose is simple—to speak only of God."

It was in Jericho, that hot flat place of boiling sands where the twelve did their first personal work. In comforting the sick they found that speaking to the soul of the afflicted resulted in healing for some. After Jericho on their way up to cooler Jerusalem, they met some seekers from Mesopotamia. Stopping their retinue, Jesus spent days with the Eastern pilgrims. When the pilgrims resumed their route along the Euphrates, singing riffs of newly learnt Hebrew tunes, they became aware of a novel state within themselves, the rare state of happiness.

Before their group reached Jerusalem, Lazarus came out from Bethany to visit their camp. Both of his parents, he related to Jesus, had joined their

## The Ordination of the Twelve

ancestors in Abraham's bosom. Lazarus offered to house the brotherhood's twelve on his large and prosperous estate. It was a manse of arched colonnades, of many chambers, clear spaces, a garden of olives, hibiscus, groves of carob and pine and scattered, of course, the gorgeous pomegranates. The house had the atmosphere of all civilized places, offering both solitude and companionship. Martha and Mary, by now both gracious and discerning women, welcomed the apostle men. As they entered the portico, all of them instantly friends, bowing lightly and turning about as in a subtle dance among the airy columns of the courtyard.

Martha had by then become a matronly girl, plump as a peony and as pretty. She was still unmarried, but busy with the hundred diversions of a pleasant domestic life. Mary, her thin, darker sister had retained the look of an abstract, vaporous waif. Only, she wasn't. Like many others who had met him, Mary too was quite "in love" with Jesus. Though not in a way her culture let her make sense of. The way Mary, (and all sorts of women—mothers, virgins, grandmothers,) loved Jesus was not an emotion most societies had a mold for. From the time Mary had met him as a child by the road in Bethany, the love she had for him felt to her quite mad. At first it had melted the grid of reason in her, seized her energy and channelled it the one way, all of it into a constant, gentle meditation on God. Mary's love for the Divine had been triggered by the integral beauty of Jesus, first as a boy and then as a man. Nor was her being "in love with God" a gift to Mary. Not knowing for years what it was, for a long time it felt crazy to her. It was a love that made Mary feel different, a difference which she knew would make her pay. Unable to give herself elsewhere, she would be alone, alone with it, an outsider because of it. Understandably, most of the people who also loved Jesus had all tried to get his attention, to declare it, to demonstrate it, to do something for him, or get him to do something for them. But Mary, who really adored his perfection, hid her love from him. She never made herself obvious, either to him, or to herself. After childhood, for the rest of his life she hardly even spoke to him. Or only cordially, and never alone, or with the slightest intent that he notice her. When she listened to him, she concealed how really and utterly ravished she was by everything he said, under a courteous smile of formal affection and a few conventional pleasantries. She lived with the love, as you could with a pain as invisible as a pulsar star. The great piety of Mary was to love, and to go on loving, with her mouth shut. If she never confided her love to anyone, it was not because she was secretive or ashamed. She simply didn't have the words for it, or know how to.

And now, as Mary, Martha and Lazarus came forward to embrace Jesus, since childhood their best friend, his Bethany friends noted in him that always awaited and now emerging quality—the splendor of a universe in a human being.

*Chapter XVI*

# This Bright Day

"What?" cried his men, each variously spooked at the sight of Jerusalem. This eerie, walled-in, haunting site at which their Master as a boy had wept with love, now caused fear in his brother men. A fortress of unnerving stone, they felt it to be a strangling place. It reeked of closure, assassins, hysteria, torture, just the spot to asphyxiate the potential of universality in the Jewish spirit. The twelve men were turning in mesmeric slow circles. Under a sky as scabby as the skin of a melon, they stepped back, halted by an encircling scene of rock terraces and lava shelves, of steeply sloping gorges and dingy ravines, the haunt of hated hyenas and leopards. Though it was the vernal season, the hills chapleting the city were bare. Ravens croaked above. The mountains around Jerusalem, much eulogized by other pilgrims, to these Galilean men looked pitiless.

"Vicious, even," groused Peter.

"Intolerant," Matthew assessed.

"Caesarean gray" scowled the young imaginative John.

The stripped hills had been torched by Rome's legionaries. Skeletons of dead pine trees hung perpendicularly between ground and sky. And that smell! Was it of burning? Rust? Blood? A nauseous whiff here of the past's multiple crucifixions, and where, but for the hand of the angel, Abraham would have made a blood-sacrifice of his son Isaac to God. "Brrrrrr." they shivered, hurrying on.

Entering the walls, the city chilled them with its charge of death. A warren of barricades and partitions, broken walls, the light on stones already at a slant of goneness. For a second an insupportable tribulation proposed itself—could the creative power of God, the Father-Son relationship that lay in Jesus be spurned here?

Sweeping aside the dread of that, they all went on and straight to the temple. Standing by its portals, they found it, too, a de-settling place. The flung blood of slain animals rang off stones. The stench of animals torn by priests' hands. The howl of slaughter echoed from the temple's giant steps. From its massive outer courts to the inner, the temple had nine gates. Women, heathens, hapless strays, and even drunks, had been stoned to death in it. In a fortress of such self-terrified enclosure, the word "Love" might sound like blasphemy. Especially if attributed to the dread Lord of the "Chosen," he, the ferocious *Ha Shem*, who, according to Scripture, was enwrathed each day with everyone, yet favored Israel, his first-born, above everyone else.

However, when Jesus went forward through the quailing listeners of that day to speak of a God who loved the crushed, the nobodies and the weak, the throngs that flocked to hear of this new thing grew so huge that they spilt outside the sacred precinct.

If Jerusalem was a symbol of the nation's yearning, so was the temple, like the Messiah, an emblem of the nation's nostalgia for itself. Not that the priests of the temple ever wanted Scripture fulfilled. For, if the true Messiah came, it would be the end the Law and of the Temple, the end of the hierarchy that upheld it, the cessation of all conflict and clash, the end, very likely, of God commanding Jews to be a nation. So, no, no ruler of Israel ever wanted the Messiah to come—what *was* wanted was the longing for him, the discontent and agitation of it. Hence the Messiah's coming had to be endless.

Now, unlike the clerics and the legion of flunkeys who depended on them, the more erudite and sceptical of Jerusalem's Jews didn't think Jesus was blasphemous. Of course not. How could a man's words, "Humans are from the divine" defile the God of Heaven? No, to sceptics the clerics were meretricious hysterics. But, deemed these sophisticates, this notion of that Jesus fellow being "God become Man," now *that* that was laughable! Downright silly, in fact. The pathos of it! The cosmic-loneliness of humanity was stripped naked by the wish-fantasy of it. As for the Galilean rascal's teachings, they were merely inurbane, even mischievous. He was misguided, perhaps even a little "touched"? But they admitted he was unique, a person with no outer-man or inner-man; he was the same both sides. So he intrigued them somewhat.

Now Annas, the high priest of the Temple, floated somewhere between these two positions. He was an elderly relative of Zebedee and his wife, Salome. Since the childhood of Jesus, Annas had watched the boy from afar, his breath held involuntarily, rapt. But Annas had been squirming with apprehension. Because, he knew it, when Jewry was to first hear Jesus, the priests of the temple would hear the beginning roar of the wave that would sweep them away. Annas knew the priests were the set that Jesus would get in trouble with. What he said would rock their authority, their obsession with sin, the blood sacrifice, the excruciation and waste of animals. Even worse, by wiping out vicious rituals, Jesus would challenge the priests for standing between God and man. He would accuse them of blasphemy; say that their pride gave God offense, that they were cruel to the poor, that they were hypocrites who stained the word "religion." Jesus would say the Father is not in the temple, nor anywhere the priests said, but in people's hearts. And by saying all this, Annas knew, Jesus would relocate the seat of human identity and power.

Yes, Annas knew all this. But he didn't personally care. A gelding intellectually, Annas wouldn't have stood on any issue. He had no convictions, no care, this way or that. His religion was of a deadening banality, just the droning, stagnant protocol of a soporific survival. The shift of power for Annas was the thing intolerable. For Jesus would shift the power. He would move it from the priests to the people, from the elite to the common, from the narrowly national to the grand planetary total. Jesus would revise the mind-set of Israel. He would change the meaning of believing, of humanity itself. Redefining who people were to God, not indebted sinners, but each one his free and dear child, Jesus would change the status of humans. And God being the Father of all, it would be the end of all mediation and of all separation, the end of priests and sects, the end of nations, religions, of special persons and places, frontiers and borders, the end of everything that ever stopped you from loving everyone else. If Jesus was right, Annas had worked it out, their whole system would collapse. But if Jesus could be shamed in the world's eyes, then the power Annas stood for would be proved right.

If Jesus was right, then Israel was wrong.

It was either him or them.

Of course he had to die.

Therefore when Jesus knocked on the door to visit his old friend, Annas, knowing even the exact pitch of that rap, lumbered forward with the grimmest reluctance. Though an old man in clutch of Jewry's highest official position, Annas was as petulant as an infant. His mouth was pinched downwards as he opened the ornate portal of his Jerusalem palace. One look at the man's retracting expression, and Jesus turned, gathering his apparel to himself.

"Fear and pride, Annas," he said to his friend, "they make a slave of a man. Are you going to lose your freedom to them?" Fully faced to the priest, he waited a moment. Then turned. And left.

Annas stood on, rigid on the threshold, saying nothing. A fixed and imperious impassibility occluding his face.

But from then on, Jesus went ahead. He went straight to the temple in Jerusalem, and when the pilgrim people heard his word they liked it so exceedingly well that it was carried from Palestine, to the edges of the Roman empire, out to the frontiers of the world.

While in Jerusalem, Jesus met a man, Jacob. He sought out Jesus in secret at the home of Flavius, the Hellenized art collector.

Facing the younger man, Jacob took position on an oriental divan. He was soliloquising at Jesus with the performing earnestness of lecturing men. "Take the holy nation," Jacob was instructing the Master, "The first age of the Hebrews saw the Divine as a force of jealousy and wrath. The next age saw God as a wreaker of vengeance. But," groaned Jacob, quite felled by the new word Jesus had, "the dread Lord of Hosts, the feared *Ha Shem*, what's this Rabbi about—God being a Father of 'Universal Love'?"

"Well said!" Jesus had most innocently enjoyed Jacob's flatfooted lecture. "But you know," he now leaned companionably toward the man, "God is changeless. It is only human ideas about God that grow. And the age is ripe for the next step. A new beauty of God, his character of a Father, his nature, love. This is good news, Jacob, no?"

Jacob protested, "But good Master, our forefathers saw God as Moses had!"

"If," said Jesus, "you insist on seeing like Moses, why have the generations struggled? In this bright hour, you can see the Father as no one before has! Jacob, God is your Father. He loves, not only the whole human family, but each individual. You love each of your own children, don't you? So, accept the love the Father has for you—not just for being Abraham's child, but for you, just for the person you are."

## This Bright Day

In Jacob a spark ignited. "I believe this. It must be just so." Jacob bowed. He was filled with a new heart, "I believe you. And I thank you," he put his hands together to the man, "my Rabbi."

In Jerusalem, for a day or two each week, Jesus stayed at the home of Flavius. His host was a lover of art. From when they first met, Jesus had asked to be shown the gallery of the collector of art. Amazed by the wall paintings, floor mosaics, the dexterously worked free standing sculptures, Jesus walked around them in thrall to the beauty, rapt. He asked to be told about the process of tinting, the firing and glazing of the exquisite ware. Flavius, the Greek, was amazed. How could a Jew, and a pious one at that, feel no disgust for art, but an emotion bordering on reverence?

"But these are works of beauty!" Jesus cried among the sculptures, his arms open, turning around. "Art speaks of the Above. The children of Moses have misunderstood what he meant. They made false gods of many foolish things, even of their own prohibition of images. But Flavius, the restrictions of those far dim times—what have they to do with this bright day when God is seen as the Lord of the Universe? Who in this age could confuse the Universal Creator with idols of stone?"

By Jesus' saying that, Flavius as a lover of art, understood; the making of art by humans was not profane, but its opposite, an act that is blessed.

While in Jerusalem, a man asked Jesus, "But Rabbi, how can we know with certainty that you are sent by God?"

Though hardly stirred to prove his identity, far less enforce it, because the question was sincere, Jesus answered, "Know the message by its fruit. If a message is genuine, the spirit in you shall witness to you. Learn how to hear it. Learn to trust it. If you receive God as your Father, you will become his child by that. If you believe God, you will know who you are. And then you shall know who I am also."

"But, my Lord," Thomas, as skeptic, joined in, "how can I know if it *is* the spirit who speaks in me, and not one of my own voices?"

"When the supreme spirit speaks to your soul its voice is unmistakable. You cannot confuse it with your own sayings to yourself. If you accept God, you will be born of his spirit. And if born of the spirit, you can overcome the wranglings of doubt by faith."

"Which is the greater; the doubt that seeks truth? Or the faith which, to feel secure, runs from it?"

"Faith" smiled Jesus, not tricked, "overcomes all."

"What's the evidence of this to the world?"

"Only one; that you love one another."

Of the many pious Jewish souls now seeking out Jesus in secret, Nicodemus was the most refined. He was an elderly member of the Sanhedrin, the body of rule in that theocratic land. Of staunch and authentic moral fibre, Nicodemus was self-developed, eager to please, discriminate. Hearing of the radical teachings of Jesus—so irksome to his colleagues while to his own ear so excellent—he stole outside Jerusalem's walls. He was headed up to the apostles' camp halfway up Mount Olivet.

Feeling foolish to be secretive, he entered the room where Jesus was. From the start, Nicodemus felt demeaned by his own sneaking; the vanity of a timid man to be so mindful of what others thought. But welcomed by Jesus, he had an intuitional flash; here was a man who had been with God's heart, and was now looking into his own. Nor in his attitude to a senior, powerful man, did Jesus have any tinge of self-deprecation, or any trace of deference. Nicodemus felt disarmed, the man wasn't doing a thing to persuade him. He leaned forward, "Good Rabbi," Nicodemus essayed, "We know you must be sent by God. For no mere man could so teach unless God were with him." Having laid his tribute, he hoped not obsequiously, at the feet of the man, the elder asked about that burning Jewish issue, The Kingdom.

"A man cannot enter it, Nicodemus," after this opening skirmish of manners, Jesus brightened to their subject, "unless he be born of the spirit. Like the wind, you cannot lay hold of it. But you can see its manifestations."

"How can this be . . . ?"

"You are a teacher in Israel, yet ignorant of this?" the younger man gently chided him, "And, were you told of Heaven's truths, Nicodemus, would you have the courage to believe?"

"How may I . . . ?"

"By believing in God's spirit. That it lives in you. If you could let yourself be led by it, you will begin to see with its eyes. Were you to desire it with a whole heart, you will be born of it. And my friend," Jesus opened his hands, "the choice is yours!"

Nicodemus looked deflated. He sat staring glumly ahead. Although he felt the most radiant of truths in this man, he sat on, stiffly formalized. In a culture fixated on dignity, seeing rigidity as honor, immovability as integrity, Nicodemus did not know how to let go of his will. For the moment, he was preferring to think he had no idea what Jesus meant when he said, people ought to believe as does a little child. Obedient to the protocol that he be a dignified, untoppled man, he did not know how to let go of a past posture of mind.

Only later would Nicodemus undo his prideful wilfulness, and allow the inrush of the faith by which to claim Jesus, and that, when others around him had fled a scene of suffering and death.

In the lording context of Jerusalem Jesus spoke of another central matter, power.

In truth he opened arms to his listeners, the word "Kingdom" was not well used in speaking of spirit. He said he regretted having to use it, implying, as it did power and its structures. Also, the authoritarian force behind "Kingdom" would have no appeal to minds that were free. Nor, he said, did it describe God's true connection to the human family. In truth, the image of a family is a far better one. The families of earth reveal the pattern of the families of heaven. As children take their existence from their parents, so is it with humans and God. Good parents take pleasure in providing for their children. They prepare and train their daughters, guide and restrain sons. Parents give loyalty, companionship. And, unlike a judge, a parent freely forgives. "Moreover," he said, "parents like to leave their children an inheritance."

"I am," hands opening, he said, "I am also a Son. That your way be made wider to God is why I have come."

At times like these, his disciples saw right into him. They could see the essence of Jesus, a man perfect before God. Their vision of him testified that this was a perfection anyone could reach. From him they felt linked to the universe of future lives, all implied in him. He made you aware of the cosmos and the mustard seed, infinity and the second, the iota and the immensity. He re-framed your present into inexhaustible potentials extending to eternity.

But he was weary by now. The clamor of the masses had exhausted him. And Jerusalem was a boiling cauldron, a fractious, captious place. All the groups were corralled into sects. The Zealots were seething fire-brands. The Essenes, Pharisees, Sadducees, all meant to be hailers of God, but in practice, shockingly stingy about their Lord. The Pharisees were all holier-than-thou, walking about in veils in order to see no evil, but still managing to look down on everyone else. The Sadducees were caustic. The Essenes, elitists. The scribes, hissy and nitpicking, the lawyers corrupt. And the public hours of daily turning himself inside-out to speak had worn Jesus out.

Not a verbose man by nature, he was actually a little tardy of speech. But it wasn't the reluctance of when you know your ideas aren't yet formed. Like most reflective people, he felt the off-center limitation of words. But knew, if he were not to evade the human and escape into cosy communing with his own divinity as did the self-congratulating mystics, he had to speak words, and he would have to work for the clarity to accurately convey his thoughts. You had to speak. Words were what you had. To find God you couldn't get away from the shared, the heard, the spoken. God was where people were. Even in the misshapen brokenness of words.

By this time, the Jerusalem establishment hated Jesus. They deplored what he said. Also, they were noting a haunting new tone, a new soul being created in the city. Not to vex matters, Jesus and his followers left. They went south to be with Abner, also a teacher in Israel, a man whom Jesus knew through his cousin, John.

Down in the south of scalding Hebron, Jesus visited Abner's colony of Nazarites. They were a community of austere ascetics. But when Jesus spoke with these pious eccentrics, his word was felt to be too simple for their highly chiselled tastes. They desired a teaching more painstaking, difficulty being the proof of a superior practice. His teaching was for children, they said. It was too general, no selectiveness about it, and hardly any effort. Even worse, the kingdom's attainment got you no distinction; there were no grades, no notches of attainment, nothing above anyone else. And the Nazarite mystics found it quite disagreeable of the man to have included no fasting in his teachings, or any of the distinguished techniques of self-mortification.

By early summer Jerusalem's ire against Jesus had ebbed. So their small band plodded back from Hebron. They lived in tents at Gethsemane, that garden slope of Mount Olivet. Below, in the bone-colored valley ran the brook of Kidron. They bathed here daily. And each Sabbath saw them with Lazarus, Martha and Mary in Bethany.

Quiet prevailed in June.

One night, a man, Joseph of Arimathea, crept to the tent where Jesus slept. He came stealthily with his friend, Nicodemus. Since meeting Jesus, Nicodemus had been changing, however indefinably. In the dark now wavered the two elders' sneaking silhouettes. They were split between fear of public condemnation and the desire to speak with this controversial teacher.

## This Bright Day

Because once again Jerusalem was buzzing about him. Once more, without meaning to, Jesus had drawn the fire of attention. He had forgiven the most vile of outcasts! Just who, fumed the righteous, was he to forgive? And who to include in his Father's kingdom just anybody? What a scandal! How dare he say God was there for the vile! For whores and lepers and scum! What a horrible insult to say the Lord of the Universe cared for these! It was a threat to decency, to the respectable, to the nation itself. Of such an opinion, in the main, was the Sanhedrin. And Joseph and Nicodemus sensibly fearing that power-faction, now struggled in debate on the slopes of Olivet. Should they to see Jesus?

Fear won. They slunk away, not then ready.

But when shortly after this, totally unexpectedly, one of the Sanhedrin's members burst out at a meeting and confessed that he not only believed, but simply loved the teachings of the Galilean, outrage, always on the simmer in that city, erupted. The Sanhedrin swung into action to arrest Jesus.

Conflict never his aim, Jesus and his twelve left. They headed for the gentile cities of Archelis and Phasaelis in the Decapolis.

An explosion of laughter! Snorts of fun! That was the first contact of these preaching Jews with the Greeks of the Decapolis. These rough and bawdy colonials of the Empire roared at what the apostles preached. Though the cawing and roaring was less derisory than just hopeless, like, who could *live* such ideals! But the pagans noted, at least these Galilean boys weren't given to the hair-splitting arrogance and haughty lecturing of the Judean Pharisees. Though spared the usual rabbinic verbal trouncing, the gentiles went on cackling. But when the subject of the Teacher came up, they made a passing nod at Jesus. Still, they brayed, still guffawed, brutish and drunk, stinking of garlic and sweat. But the apostles went on against the heckling, trying to deliver the much-too-quiet-sounding message.

Howled down, they slunk back to Jesus. When settled together, Philip said, "The gentiles say our teaching is only for the poor, for the weak, for slaves. Feebleness, they say, is what we teach. Though you, Master, they like! They say you are ideal. Even heavenly. But they say, humans can't live like that. What to say to them, O Master?"

"I tell you," he smiled his calm, blue-sea-smile into the torch-lit night, "they do not yet know the power of the love by which the universes are steered. But one day they shall. Sometime they will know love is the force that moves all reality. As for you, my hawks," he burst at them, laughing, "are you still fledglings? Well?" Still roaring, he opened his arms, "are you?

## His Real Life

Look! Listen! Was John the Converter weak? Do you see me a slave to fear? As for our message being for the poor, well it's true; the poor are having the good news said to them. But I tell you, my children, the poor will be the first to accept they are the children of God. And yours is the supreme adventure of all time, the ascent through your own efforts to Paradise! What's going to be tougher or braver than that? Truly, I tell you, to die in battle surrounded by comrades is easy. But to serve your spirit asks for more courage than any brazen act. Many of you will die for loyalty to it. And no army will display more valor than you as you speak your convictions to the world. You will astonish all by the courage it takes to live out your highest lights."

Newly inspired, each man promised himself—speak from now with a new dominance of spirit.

Courage, they were learning, was self-control for a human. When reviled, Jesus never hit back. When he suffered, he made no threats. When finally denounced, he simply commended himself to Heaven's Father with a human heart's quiet brokenness.

"And now," said he, "Let us go into Samaria."

The Decapolis defeat had flattened them. If the gentiles had been abrasive, the Samaritans, blood-sworn enemies of the Jews, might provide a worse drubbing than that. Rejection with scorn was one thing; but the shrug of indifference could shrivel. The apostles were men raised to prevail, used to subduing others, bossing women, dictating to children. And now they were beginning to see, there could be ages of personal refusal, long stretches of rejection, years and years of the energy going nowhere, perhaps a life-time of futile, unavailing effort. They had never considered the possibility of failure, of the love un-received, the vision flagging, heart taken out of it. Direction athwart, aims gone fuzzy, they hung about inert.

On this past preaching tour, the apostle Andrew had been a knot of problems; John had been perplexed. James was troubled. Peter, overwrought. And Judas was having a sensitivity fit. Thomas was slumped in a depression, Philip was nonplussed. Nathaniel, the worst for him, was humorless. And Simon Zealotes was sputtering on again about the sons-of-the-Devil that meant anyone outside Judaism. Only the twins Alpheus were cheery and normal.

Surging forward the next morning with a smart clap of his hands Jesus roared to them, "Before we go to Samaria, let us go for a three day hike to Mount Sartaba!"

## This Bright Day

Apprehension—usually the spawn of imagination—can be put aside, or so they discovered as they beat their way up Mount Sartaba. At the start, everyone was sullen. But bit by bit they slid into jokes, teasing one another, flipping helping arms over ledges, hoicking toes and torsos over gaps, jibbing each other as they went. Their movement through the scrub with the swifts and rock doves flying about, cut the men loose to drift along in nature's verdure. In the wide amplitudes of that land, its classic shades and juicy green spread they were freed from torpor and vacancy, delivered from silliness and self. Tramping on into the late afternoon, hills emerged before them, and sank, the land buckled in a heap, then quelled in a roll, sloping down, dividing, circling as they went. A whole day of muscular heft and hardly mentioning a snip of worry, their rambling recovered their perspective.

Then they gained Sartaba's top. Here they stopped. Looking around, they saw swathes of grass, the land below, the turquoise escarpments to the side, vertiginous, down-plunging bronze folds, pink bluffs and gristly elevations. Out there on the edge of a cliff was the horizon's magical curve upon their powder-blue earth, extensive, spacey, and beautiful below. They snatched embarrassed looks at each other.

And burst out laughing.

After a deep snoring night, next day they were ringed by Samaria's sonorous mountainscape beauty. Settling to it, they reminisced of things past. Still later, with energy recovered, some fell to cavorting and pranking, and out came their raucous, raving, playful old selves. They were all slip-sliding, galumphing youths again, horsing around. Still later, whittling a new staff, or cooking the edibles found, they told stories to each other about their children, and of friends, or a cat somebody had, or just horsed around.

Even Judas, a man chronically withdrawn into unnecessary hurt and coiled tight upon his own meanings, uncurled at that evening's sight—lilac volutes of light smote the earth and ran along the valley's floor turning the land into fields of fire. From being a man who really and shamefully suffered, when Judas saw the light run over the valley, turning donkeys, trees, sheep and huts into ruby statues of themselves, he felt his anguish shunt into a beauty so objective that all his hurt was snuffed out completely, but for a minute. Snared up into that mountain's brilliance, Judas had a whole moment with Jesus standing there beside him, when he knew; up here, in the total, matters were good. But despite his Brother-friend's presence close by his shoulder, his awareness of this blessing was abstract. It was of mind alone. And only for a minute. And the aesthetic having neither love nor person in it, Judas, too blunted by himself, did not feel even a wisp of the cosmic in it.

That night. When they ate, they noted, Jesus said no formal grace for their meal. No, but their every ravenous bite was that. Among the pillowy rocks on which they lolled, around them, the plump and furry hyrax, they were too mute with the happiness of being who and where they were. And to have him, have him there, to have him be with them, him, Jesus, their brother-man, and also to be there with one another, enjoying the various characters they were. Slowly on came the night. Into the deep dark they each crept, stretching and yawning, and slept. The high fields and mountains went quiet.

But in just a little while the coal black sky cracked. It burst to an invisible choir of stridulating, chirping, croaking creatures. And next, they were up, rumpled and running, each man, wide awake, bounding towards their plateau's rocky edge. And when at dawn they looked out upon mountains looping away into an acid blue infinity and saw atoms of new light dance in the shiny halls of space, they knew again: not everything came from man.

There was a creation we did not make.

And this was it!

This!

*Chapter XVII*

# Until Him

Refreshed, next day Jesus said, "Let's go to Scythar."
It wouldn't be easy. That Jews and Samaritans hated each other was a fact. No Jew ever went there, preferring tedious detours to avoid the odium of Samaria. But loyalty to him let his apostles, otherwise always ready to fume and grizzle, make their way quite docilely to the desert city of Scythar. Off to purchase provender, they left him; it was by a well where women came to draw water.

Her name was Nalda. She had always been flighty—perhaps that was the worst of her. Not a bad or stupid woman, but her talk was scatty, skimming, she wouldn't settle on anything. Her focus diffuse, it skipped from thing to thing. She kept her mind from thinking, would never consider who she was.

A pleasing, plump, placid woman with a wryly complicit little smile, Nalda paid a passing due to the customs, her chat ever ready and pat. But that anything specific, unmixed or extraordinary might have been meant for her, well, that never stayed long in her head, busy with the incidentals of the lentils, a new pair of sandals, the village jokes and gossip as she was.

A few years of beatings by her first man, his camel-betting, then the wine-stupors of that woman-walloping idiot; she would have put up with the drudge of it, just out of lethargy. But no, her first stinker of a husband dumped her. She had no kinsfolk to take care of her; she was used to someone else taking care. Unprepared to think it through—that look, yes, though only a woman, you *can* survive in a modest, if exerted existence. She had heard of other kinless women doing weaving, growing mushrooms, pasturing goats up North in the highlands. She could have cultured those profitable berries, sold them at market, the tomatoes and the lucrative hyssop, or started an enterprise with goat's wool perhaps. But to that world, a self-directed woman was a witch, a vixen, an animal; anyway, she couldn't be bothered, it was too hard. So she went to live with the next passing man who wanted her. When that turned sour, she went with a second, then a third, and—what the hell—the next. She passed from man to man, not even from the vanity of wanting to be wanted, but slack by habit, flinched away any chance to face herself. Too soon deciding her soul would never be met, she gave up early on what hungered in her. But her avoidance stayed as intense as an ache, and she wouldn't look at it, or not too much, and some expedient man was always easier.

Until him.

In the red-bronze sundown of a Samaritan mountain evening she had gone to the well. About to draw the water for the night, she bent over the rim of the well. She saw him from a corner of her awareness even before she lifted her eyes to him. When she did, she thought she recognized him. He came out of a dream across the haze of her mind, the absurdly beautiful and disciplined body of a barbarian king, the fall and spring of sun-streaked hair, those blue-green eyes that some Jews had, and that slant of light, or whatever it was that came from him to her. But she brushed it, like everything too acute, under the veil of her mind's conventions.

Sure, he was a Jew, and, she saw with a gaudy blush, what a man! But alas, however fetching as a woman, she was only a Samaritan. And if truth be told, she cracked a dismissive little snarl at herself, a bit of a slut—well, at one remove. Anyway, one such as he, a man of such steady gaze, what verve in that muscled stance, his shoulders' span—well, she shrugged, subsiding—he was a Jew and obviously devout. He would hardly look at *her*. Let alone speak!

But he did.

"Give me to drink," leaning against the well he spoke with that level, unhurried voice she knew he would have.

"How," she struck up in her flirtatious mode, "How is it that you, a Jew, ask for a drink from a Samaritan woman?"

## Until Him

He looked her in the eye. "I have indeed asked you for a drink. But if you could hear me aright, you would ask me for a draught of the living waters of life."

Some long ago part of Nalda snapped back to reality at that. But dreading it too, her mind skittered off sideways, and besides, she wanted to manage this. So she was persuading herself, that he, being such a man, and she, being so attracted to him, he was awakening to her. "But sir," she was lisping coyly, "you have nothing to draw with, where have you this living water?"

"Everyone," he was austere, "who drinks of this water shall thirst again. But whoever drinks the water of the living spirit shall never thirst."

Hearing that, her head went light. Nalda stood awash in a visual-dream of water. There was a flash of her long buried craving being at last and eternally met. But no, she decided, no, he couldn't possibly, he was too desirable, she wanted him, and yet, how strange, not in that way, but anyway, she hung back now, confused. Resorting to her well-stropped flirting, she swaggered, "Well then. Give it to me. And besides, anything a Samaritan woman could receive from a Jew like you would be a pleasure."

He looked her level in the eye. And Nalda knew it; she had made a woeful mistake.

"Woman," he said, "go, get your husband, bring him here."

She reeled. It was not so much at the embarrassment of her error, as with the terror of her first thought returning, of this event being the confrontation of her whole life. "Sir," she murmured, "I have no husband."

"It would be better if you would not trifle with my words," he replied, "but seek the living water I offer you."

Instead of walking off, his words were letting her through to his meaning. For the first time in ages, she felt the sting of honest shame for the evasions of the past, the issues of her soul she had slunk away from, preferring ease and flippancy. "My lord," she bent, one hand touched to her brow, "I repent my manner of speaking to you, I did not perceive . . ."

As she lifted her eyes, his shape by the well happened to eclipse the evening sun. And she was about to ask the first real question of her life from this man, a man as pure as God. But just as this possibility appeared to her, that yes, the Creator *could* be in a man as good and present as the Creation itself, her mind baulked, and scurried back to her base-line response, to save herself. Pointing to Mount Gerizim, she went on chatting, "Our fathers have worshipped on this mountain for ages; would you say it is on Gerizim or in Jerusalem they ought to worship?"

When he looked at her, she knew it; she had side-stepped it, yet again, this chance for her soul to make contact with reality.

But when he spoke, his voice was kind. "Woman, let me say to you, it doesn't matter where you worship the Father, Mount Gerizim or Jerusalem. Your salvation will come not from knowing how or where others worship, but by receiving into your heart the living waters I am offering you,"

She could have met him, or, what was much the same thing, she could have come to herself. But neurotically stuck now, she ducked yet again, chirping on, "Oh yes, I know sir. John preached about the Converter, the One who will turn us . . . "

He stopped her. "Nalda." he said, "I, who speak to you, am he."

It was the first time he had given it voice. The first time he said it to anyone. And she knew it felt like something never in all time said. That he first revealed who he was to a woman, and to a Samaritan, and to one of questionable character, took Nalda so far beyond herself that the entire panorama of her life convulsed. About to ask her life's first question about God, she opened her mouth, just when the men in his company came trooping back to the well. His apostles, a band of brother-men, were shocked at the sight of their Master speaking to a woman. Who at least was bowed, showing respect.

As if in a gale indeed, Nalda's body was bent. One arm covering her form, the other hung loose, she stood athwart. It was the worst of her life's mishaps. Her one chance to hear truth was over. But he took pity on her lost moment. "Nalda," he spoke quickly to her, "God has forgiven you. You *have* received the living water. You will have a new life. Joy shall spring up in your soul. From now you shall become a daughter of the Most High."

Nalda unbent. She had no words. Numb, she only bowed to the man. Her face vague, she left the well, forgetting her water pot, and ladle, just leaving them there. She walked away, receding from the past, away from a long dodged self and into the miracle of a new life beginning its quiet streaming in her like that last, thin, hardly palpable flow of pink in Samaria's sky.

Afterwards, she was heard to say in her village, "I met a man who told me all I ever was."

Nalda tried telling the story to her neighbors, about this man. How his presence, pointing to God, had made her want to face herself. She tried saying how, through him, she saw who she was. Yes, she tried, but after a life of prattle and gabble, of habituated cliché, she couldn't verbally convey it, or not properly, and her friends couldn't be bothered; they were bored by her and busy. But it didn't matter at all; for Nalda had already started her way to it.

*Chapter XVIII*

# Holy Land
## The Apostle's Epilogue

For all of Samaria's receptive affection, Jerusalem was waiting in him like a fate. The summers of Scythar were scalding. So this motley, unimportant little entourage was scaling up against the shelving slopes to pitch their tents high in the cool of Samaria's legendary Mount Gerizim.

Night fell. Ringed about by rocks, the group sat by a fire of briers. They were tired. Lounging about on the stones, they stared exhausted into the flames. Some of the men were looking about for him, craning necks, feeling inadmissibly lost when he wasn't with them. But then there he was, his shape parting the dark. He was coming through, gathering them, saying, "Come, come along, come."

When they were all together, he began to speak. "Take," he said, "the suffering in any person's life . . . it might be a fact, long or short, but even affliction is a great value if understood. The values by which one person lives are the central truth about any woman or man, not what befalls them, not even a grievous end."

When he spoke, behind the warmth and steadiness of a mature man, he seemed to them to be suffering himself. Socially he was still out and lone, taking no refuge in confecting honorific roles for himself, living neither by precept or law, only by poetry and an undefended tenderness. And, some of his ideas still seemed vague to those who wanted a fixed program, for the teachings to be inflexibly targeted to a specific goal. If he, too, seemed to suffer from tremendousness himself, wasn't it because he was for the whole of life? And that his own human mind could not fully encompass the infinity on which it was launched?

Though his theme was the Infinite, he sought the ground of it in his men. Now among the mountains, he was inviting them to say what they would about God. They asked, "How should we see him?"

"As a father," he said. "The Universal Creator is known abroad the universe by many names. The name a creature gives to God signifies the relationship that is felt. At your own present phase on earth, the word 'Father' is best."

From their spread around the fire, someone, probably Philip, piped up, "And what about you, Master? How do we see you?"

"As a brother," he smiled, "see me as a brother, a friend."

Another night, still in the region of Scythar, they wanted to talk about worship.

Unexpectedly, he said, "Let your worship be through your contact with material reality." Then, with a lyrical tinge in his voice, "Worship is the looking of the one for the inspiration of service to the many. Worship is the part identifying with the whole, the finite with the Infinite . . . it is time in the act of striking step with eternity. Worship is a child talking with the Father, an assumption of refreshing, creative attitudes by the soul. And let me say this, you know that fearful feeling many people have of isolation in the universe—there is always a remedy! Do this one thing only; remember God. That is all. When in distress, just say in yourself " . . . Father, Father . . ."

At times like these, they felt their relationship to the Father lay in Jesus. With him they remembered God. He was the restorer of the memory of God. The way he was a son to the Father was how they were too.

Later that evening when he finished speaking, of those by the fire, a few had the sense that even if they hadn't fully grasped all he said, those of other worlds might, and the generations to come certainly would.

By now it was late. Jesus stood up. He stretched. With a fond gesture to everyone he turned. Weary now, he was off to sleep. As they watched him move off into the night with the all but invisible tread of a man of no pride, each man experienced his own truth of him. Though each man felt who Jesus was, each with a personally appropriate impression of him, as a group, they knew: from this point on, their Master would enter the wider public phase of his life.

He walked into the dark alone, a man, receding into the olive groves. Blurred a shade by weariness, his friends slid into a meandering chat. His appearance, somebody remarked, didn't he now look like a man entirely engulfed by the divine? Yes, they said, yes, as in their time with him they had seen the divine over-spread the human part in Jesus, not erasing or subduing, but enlarging it. Someone asked, what about his dual nature? What was the meaning of heaven being in a man? And, did divinity's out-spread go further than the man? For, if holiness was passed into Jesus, did it not fan out to humanity? And from the humans to our surrounds of nature, the environment of our bodies? What about the ground he walked? The rocks he touched? The sky he saw, the animals, the trees and those five sparrows known, of course, to God?

They talked about it. This land was his geographic context, his physical matrix. The history of Palestine had grown around him; it moved with him, shaping him with its events of climate, custom, habit and governance, all of these jostling him about. So this land had to have gone into him, at least to some extent. More importantly, if a man's holiness could grow out of organic matter, did holiness perhaps also go back into it, sanctifying it?

So, into the night they went on imagining . . .

Was this, the physical land he walked, were these, the waters he fished and rode, these hills and deserts where he came to consciousness, the seeds and the vineyards, the tares, the darnel, and those sempiternal sparrows he loved so well, what about them? Weren't these, too, holy?

This Palestine had been so called by Romans after the Philistines, the enemies of Jews, as a mockery. So the apostles wondered, might this land one day be called after the name their forefather, Jacob, had won from his wrestle with the angel at Peniel? This land, to be called Israel, had been made holy by his coming to it. And though each man present was a fervid Jew, they had to face this one; their Lord by now was not just a Jew, nor just a man, nor was he just his mother's or his country's son. He had left behind those bonds of identity and belonging long ago. He had shed those partial selves to become, as must they, Universal Man. So if God's holiness radiated into Jesus, and from him into the land, then, (Now they had to not fall over this one, but vault over themselves, and fly!) then, the function of holiness was to spread out from Israel to every nook and cranny of the earth, and, for all they knew, to then, rarely conceivable multiplicity of galaxies beyond.

*Holy Land*

So they went on musing, guessing. If his presence blessed every pebble on Jewish soil, did it not mean that, (he being a link between spirit and matter,) every pebble on every other soil was blessed?

Could this be the real meaning of Holy Land?

That the divine came to the human here had made of this earth a place of sacredness. If this land was a font of holiness, did it not spread into other lands and peoples? By blessing the existence of all places and races, Israel pointed away from itself. This was Israel's real consecration, its long, prophetic offering-up. In the broad light of a God who sent his spirit to all, Israel was no longer a nation existing only for itself. It was no longer just a place or a race living only for its own dreams and ambitions for itself. Holy Land was the planetary point that spread the blessing by pointing away from itself. Scripture, they recalled, had God telling the Jews to be a light to the nations. But did not the bringer of light have to become as light itself, invisible and perceived only by its effects? Transcendence, as prophesied by Scripture, might still be the destiny of Israel's people after all.

As they spoke on about these things, they had presentiment of their Lord as being their land, thunderous and rocky, but once watered, its yield was miraculous. Watching his back recede, to their eyes his movement into the night was as the radiant wake of the land's beauty vanishing into the dark. From the hardly audible footfall of his step, and the surrendered angle of his head, they saw at last; his was the tremendous suffering of a man never fully met. At his going into the night, panic brushed the skin of each man. In the past, when Jesus left them, for a day, or for a minute, even only for the purposes of nature, they felt orphaned. Though fully grown men, most of them married and fathers of children, when he left them, they felt jilted, abandoned. Watching his form being absorbed into the night, they admitted a childish thing: they had felt parented, mothered and fathered, when with him. One to the other, they admitted, his was a presence to cause the icy separation of space to thaw. When with him, duration was suspended, friction ceased, material force was cancelled. He made time melt into perpetual tenderness. And when he looked at you with those sky-clear eyes he launched the completest silence in souls. His words caused the purest wave of love to rush into hearts and when he looked at you, you felt known at last, and forgot the failures, the griefs and defeats of the past. And although you were known by him, he was a man never to be fully known. Only his Father could know him. But his Father who knew him was afar, in Heaven, and he was here, on earth, isolated by who he was. He could never be loved for what he was, since nobody could know all of him. The awful fact, they realized with alarm, was that any human being could be better loved than him; for anyone else could be understood, at least in potential, by another.

So, they who loved him as much as they could, sensed how he suffered from that. They knew what his humanity suffered; ultimately and necessarily, the love unreturned.

The fewest of times, and almost in passing, he had mentioned his loneliness, spoken of homelessness, of nowhere to lay his head. He was cut off from others by what he was, starting with his one need of humans, love and truth.

His was the solitude of the un-comprehended man, the love so complete as to never be understood on earth.

www.ingramcontent.com/pod-product-compliance
Lightning Source LLC
Chambersburg PA
CBHW051101160426
43193CB00010B/1265